Praise for Step U.
for Emerging Leaders

"It takes the initiation of an idea by a single person to open windows of possibilities to enhance our lives. The quotations Karanne has shared in *Step Up* are not simply beautiful words but rather they are words that serve as lampposts along the way of our journey through life. Through the words of quotes, Karanne shares a deeper meaning inside each quote and how it can be applied to our own lives through 52 weekly exercises she created. I recommend to anyone who is searching for inspiration. I have thoroughly enjoyed it."

Mary Morrissey, International Speaker, Best-Selling Author, CEO Consultant, Visionary, Empowerment Specialist

"I have just read five chapters of Karanne's new book, and I can't wait to read the rest. Karanne is a well-respected Health Information Management professional and the insights and self reflections she is sharing will be inspirational to young professionals wanting to move into leadership positions."

Gail Crook, CEO & Registrar, Canadian Health Information Management Association

"I am excited and happy for Karanne who has followed her dream in sharing her life's 'wisdom' with you in this book. I have had the wonderful gift of being a colleague and friend and have observed her in her conviction in meeting her goals. Through these 'teachings' I am confident you will too."

Kathleen Addison, Senior Provincial Director, Health Information Management

"Step Up is an essential life skills manual that will elevate your personal mastery of leadership."

Laurel Geise, inspirational author, speaker and Founder of The Geise Group, www.LaurelGeise.com

"Karanne Lambton's book *Step Up: 52 Actions for Emerging Leaders* is a must have book for anyone who wants to make a significant change and become a great leader. The book is easy to follow and gives you a week by week list of to-do's, not just theory, which I find very impressive."

Judy O'Beirn, Creator of International best-selling series *Unwavering Strength,* **www.unwaveringstrength.com**

"This insightful gem will, inspire your thoughts and trigger your actions. Ultimately, shifting your leadership into gear."

Colleen Evans, Enduring Leader in Health

"This book is full of words of wisdom to move through your personal and professional life with greater ease. It makes you think; it motivates you to take action; it promotes growth. The quotes and insights are uplifting and inspirational yet on a deep level, it might seem like something new yet there is a "knowing" that it speaks the truth. As an entrepreneur, this is a book that I plan to read and re-read as it will present different insights when I am in a different place in life. Thank you, Karanne, for a book that can assist people to do what they love, making their life more fulfilling and the world a better place."

Annette M. Buchanan, Owner Boxwood Manor (a 225 family farm and venue for life's celebrations) TheBoxwoodManor.com

"Karanne has written an insightful and delightfully simple guide to bring out the 'Leader' in the reader. Her format, peppered with personal examples, questions and actions, provides a concrete basis for self-reflection and motivation...no more fear, intimidation or blame!"

Linda G. O'Bryant, Consultant, Forevermore

"Karanne has had a direct presence and influence in my career. She has an innate ability to bring out the best in others by offering simple, yet effective tools of self exploration and inspiration. Her passion and guidance has helped me become a more self-aware, energized and inspired leader within the workplace and beyond."

Karen Brule, Healthcare Leader

"No matter how large or small your business, Karanne Lambton's *Step Up* will help you develop and refine essential leadership qualities. Indeed, if you diligently apply her *52 Actions,* you will not only become a better leader, but a better individual and a better member of society. Our world needs more people of that caliber!"

Laura Shortridge, President, Crystal Lake Solutions, LLC, Author, Speaker, Editor

"Step Up is a powerful, transformational tool for any new leader! Karanne shares personal experiences in a non-intimidating and relatable way to support and inspire new leaders. In addition, Karanne offers simple yet profound techniques that can be used by leaders at any level in order to move from hesitancy and fear right into action!"

Katherine Augustine, Esq., Speaker, Minister & Coach, MagicMakerCoaching.com

Step Up: 52 Actions for Emerging Leaders

Shared Experience and Simple Tools

Karanne Lambton, CHIM, CLMC

Foreword by Peggy McColl

Published by
Hasmark Publishing
1-888-402-0027

Cover Design, NZ Graphics

www.nzgraphics.com

Layout Ginger Marks DocUmeant Designs

www.DocUmeantDesigns.com

First Edition, 2015

ISBN13: 978-0-9920116-5-9

ISBN10: 0992011655

DEDICATION

I t would take you years to Google these compact, practical and inspiring tools that I now place in your hands. I am sharing my favorite collection of principles and wisdom that if unpreserved, would be inaccessible to younger generations. I have personally tested every action, the valuable experiences and measurable growth they brought in my development as a leader. I am dedicated to the many leaders and peers I have worked with throughout my own career, all of whom believed in me, supported me as an emerging leader and most of all trusted me to do the right thing when faced with the lessons we all need to learn. They trusted me more than I trusted myself, and that inspired me countless times to dig deep and take action for the greater good. It is my intention to share this wisdom, many tools and recommended actions with you.

Contents

Praise for Step Up: 52 Actions for Emerging Leaders . . . . . . a

DEDICATION iii

ACKNOWLEDGEMENTS ix

FOREWORD xi

INTRODUCTION xv

Chapter 1: Choosing To Lead 1

    Week 1: Desire and Discontent 3

    Week 2: Vision 5

    Week 3: Trust Yourself 7

    Week 4: Invest in Yourself.. 9

    Week 5: Choice.. 11

    Week 6: Take Action 13

    Week 7: Opportunity.. 16

Chapter 2: Listen and Learn 19

    Week 8: Listen... 21

    Week 9: The Gift of the Negative..................................... 23

    Week 10: Feedback 25

    Week 11: Stress 27

    Week 12: No Easy Answer 30

    Week 13: Worry... 32

    Week 14: Value 34

Chapter 3: Energize Yourself and Others 37

    Week 15: Confidence.. 39

    Week 16: Take Action... 42

Week 17: Do It!...44

Week 18: Accountability 46

Week 19: Attitudes..49

Week 20: Personal Motivation...51

Week 21: Contribution 54

Week 22: Truth 56

Week 23: Teamwork 58

Week 24: Supporting Others 60

Week 25: Failure 62

Chapter 4: Meeting Challenges. 65

Week 26: Trouble Ahead 67

Week 27: Priorities..70

Week 28: Perception 72

Week 29: Perfection 74

Chapter 5: Achieve Results 77

Week 30: Doing the Right Thing......................................79

Week 31: Productivity 81

Chapter 6: Your Comfort Zone. 83

Week 32: Decisions 85

Week 33: Courage 87

Chapter 7: Change 89

Week 34: Change...91

Week 35: Flexibility...93

Week 36: The Magic In Acceptance 95

Chapter 8: Develop Yourself 97

Week 37: Common Sense 99

Week 38: Experience..101

Week 39: Skills..103

Week 40: Self Awareness 105

Week 41: Open Mindedness...107

Week 42: Persistence...109

Week 43: Happiness...111

Week 44: In Your Control 113

Week 45: Health 116

Week 46: It's a Marathon, Not a Sprint...........................118

Week 47: Gratitude 120

Chapter 9: LOVE YOUR LIFE as a LEADER. 121

Week 48: Thoughts Move Into Form 123

Week 49: Imagination...124

Week 50: Forgiveness..126

Week 51: Patience 129

Week 52: Success...131

Closing Thoughts: 133

ABOUT THE AUTHOR 135

ACKNOWLEDGEMENTS

I live in deep gratitude for Mary Morrissey, *LifeSoulutions,* and my partners in believing, who have given me support while I faced my own false beliefs about my abilities and with that support I bravely moved toward my dream of becoming a published author on the Best Sellers List.

Peggy McColl shared her insights and experience with me as an aspiring author, ensuring I saw the path to publishing and getting this book into your hands.

My friend Kathryn holds my gratitude for encouraging me to take the time to add my personal experiences to support the lessons shared.

And I delight in my good fortune to have Marty and Dana who stand in support of me in everything I do.

FOREWORD

FOREWORD BY PEGGY McCOLL, NEW YORK
TIMES BEST SELLING AUTHOR

Whether you are a leader or not you will find inspiration in this fabulous book by Karanne Lambton! When Karanne shared her manuscript with me I was blown away. I love this book! For years and years I have found inspiration in quotes. It only takes a few words of wisdom and your entire outlook on life can change. And, more importantly if you follow the wisdom in the words, your results can skyrocket.

Many years ago I connected with a powerful quote by Henry David Thoreau that goes like this: "If one advances confidently in the direction of his dreams, and endeavors to live the life which he has imagined, he will meet with a success unexpected in common hours."

This short quotation is packed full of powerful words, and when followed, it truly is a formula that will help you create and sustain a positive emotional state that will bring about all that you desire.

Let's look at the elements involved:

If you advance, you're taking action and moving forward. You're actually creating new habits. Every single day you can move toward your goal through action. It doesn't matter whether you're taking small steps or giant leaps forward, as long as you're making progress.

If you advance <u>confidently</u>, you're in one of the strongest states of being that is possible. Confidence is a deeply powerful emotion, and it's within everyone. All you need to do is acknowledge that it's there and begin to experience what it would feel like to be confident—and then be it! Confidence is a muscle that becomes strong when exercised. If you have trouble feeling it, use your imagination to practice having this emotion, and it will become easier to keep your confidence switch in a high position.

If you advance confidently in the <u>direction of your dreams</u>, you're aware of where you're headed. I have been known to say, "If you don't like where you're going, change direction." People have a tendency to go one way and then another, wishing for what they want and then turning their mind in a different direction and thinking about what they don't want. As soon as you start thinking about what's undesirable to you, you direct the universe's attention away from your dreams and prevent yourself from moving forward toward your goals. Consider if your actions are taking you in the direction you want to go and whether your thoughts are leading you there as well. Get in the habit of speaking the words and feeling the emotions that will keep you going on the right path.

If you <u>endeavor to live the life you've imagined</u>, you actively picture what it will be like when you have what you truly desire. Think about your dream all the time, and feel what it will be like to lead such a life. Visualize yourself already in possession of your goals. Get in touch with the emotions that you'll experience—all of them—and do so often. Endeavoring to live the life you've imagined means acting as if you've already achieved your aims. You can begin this now, no matter how far away your goal may seem.

<u>You'll meet with a success unexpected in common hours</u> because you can't know the form or the timing of the success you'll achieve. When you're following the "formula" in Henry David Thoreau's quotation, you absolutely will meet with positive results. The universe knows no other way to respond than to provide you with that which you desire. However, the unexpected aspect of success is the "how" and "when." You don't need to know how or when it will materialize—that's up to the universe to decide. Your job is to choose your goal, advance forward, take action, be confident, and know that the way to your dream will be revealed to you when the timing is right.

In fact, the wisdom contained in Henry David Thoreau's quotation is so powerful that I recommend that you copy it and post it in a location where it will be visible to you every day. Read it often, and consider carrying it with you. Remind yourself of the powerful message behind the words. Get into the habit of following Thoreau's formula.

In the beginning of this book Karanne wrote: "It would take you years to Google these compact, practical and inspiring tools that I now place in your hands." It won't take you years as you now have this resource in your hands. My recommendation is that you allow it to become your Life Manual and buy copies for everyone you care about. You will be glad you did and they will be glad you did. May you be blessed with an abundance of success!

Peggy McColl

INTRODUCTION

I began this book one Saturday morning while I was tidying up my home office. I have had a collection of quotes for many years, some on a corkboard in front of me as I sit at my desk, some on scraps of paper stuffed in the desk drawer, some in a folder labeled 'articles to write.' As I prepared to tuck them away in a non-descript folder I wondered what it was that compelled me to collect and keep them like dear friends. What I realized is that every one of these quotes resonates in me because of its relationship to the lessons I learned throughout my career. It is my joy to pass these gems on to you.

Here is how I recommend you use this book—I have selected quotes that relate mostly to my early years as an emerging leader and I will share examples of my experiences, the choices I made, what I learned, and the skills I developed that had a measurable impact on my career.

When I began writing this book, it was going to be a simple book of quotations I had gathered that I could share with others. However, once I had gathered and sorted the quotations and reflected on what they mean to me, I realized I needed to share my own learning related to these. This then begged me to pose the question and action I challenge you with in each chapter.

I have always supported people to step into their leadership with more anticipation than hesitation. There are many paths to success but none more rewarding in life than your own path of learning as a leader.

There is great power in remembering lessons learned through your career and by bringing your learning to a level of conscious awareness that you can easily access. Your "inner leader" will make wise choices and expertly navigate your path. You may accelerate your own leadership learning cycle by reading the quote and reflecting on its meaning, addressing the question(s) posed and taking the action associated with each week's topic. These quotes will elevate you beyond your circumstances each week.

If you read one chapter per week, you will have spent a year on developing yourself as a leader. I invite you to take time to celebrate your expansion and growth as a leader, your new awareness and insights, and the actions you have taken on your journey.

Chapter 1:
Choosing To Lead

"Don't ask yourself what the world needs; ask yourself what makes you come alive. And then go and do that. Because what the world needs is people who have come alive." —Harold Whitman

D id you know that we can access our deepest motivation by noticing both what we desire and what causes us discontent? When the longing or discontent becomes so loud that even our overactive, multitasking, preoccupied brains can hear the roar, we need to act. The attention our subconscious is seeking is to have us express ourselves more fully. We find ourselves feeling a greater need to participate, a greater need to learn and a greater need to share in order to derive the harmony we seek for our soul and the satisfaction we feel from our work.

YOUR QUESTION THIS WEEK: What pain, longing or discontent have you noticed that is driving your desire to become a leader?

Examples: Wanting to double your income, making a difference in your profession or in a global community, being unhappy with the current manager, wanting to be promoted, wanting to relocate to another city, completing an advanced degree, etc.

YOUR ACTION STEP: Write two columns on a sheet of paper; one for a list of what you currently want more of and the second column for what you want less of in your work experience. Write this without allowing thoughts of any limitations of time, education or money you many think you have. This inventory will guide you. Use it to bring your focus and energy onto what you want more of and invite new possibilities with open arms.

When I made both of my lists, I felt a sudden release of great energy and enthusiasm. I felt like the "discontent" became a great friend instead of a dreaded foe of unhappiness with my current situation and I embraced the driving need for change. As an emerging leader, I became aware that rather than focusing on the negative, I needed to focus on what I wanted more of, bringing my heart to my work and creating an environment where I could more generously collaborate to achieve shared goals. As I shifted inside, my world reflected it and other members of our team shifted their own perspective in pursuing their work through partnership. This inspired a positive environment that would better meet everyone's needs.

> *"There came a time when the risk to remain tight in the bud was more painful than the risk it took to blossom." —Anais Nin*

WEEK 2: VISION

"The vision that you hold and impress upon your mind will determine what you are in harmony with . . . and whatever you are in harmony with, will be magnetized to you." —Mary Morrissey

What we hold in our mind shapes our future. Most of us hold too small a vision for our lives. We think of our lives based on current conditions rather than what we dream our future could look like. The larger and clearer the vision, the bigger, better and more effective the ideas will be that will flow into your consciousness regarding steps to take to create it in form. Build upon what you wrote last week in your 'want more of' list.

We are not limited by our past; our history does not define our future. When we have a vision we believe in, we can take baby steps or giant leaps toward the better self and better life that we see for ourselves. This week we will create the first few steps.

YOUR QUESTION THIS WEEK: If everything you desire were possible, what will your career as a leader look like three years from now?

Examples: own your own 7-figure business; be the CFO or CEO of your current company; be a renouned author and speaker; create a culture where your team can't wait to come to work every day.

YOUR ACTION STEP: Set the timer and sit quietly for 5 minutes. Allow yourself to imagine your ultimate career experience.

What does it look like, feel like, sound like? Now, write down 3 simple, bullet point action steps you can take to move toward your vision?

When I did this process, I was surprised at how easy it was to envision myself as a speaker, author and coach. My bullet points were 1) write a book, 2) be certified by a world class training organization and 3) find a mentor that has walked the path before me.

> *"Great ideas need landing gear as well as wings."*
> *—C.D. Jackson*

WEEK 3: TRUST YOURSELF

"You must train your intuition—you must trust the small voice inside you, which tells you exactly what to say, what to decide." —Ingrid Bergman

Trust your own instinct. It is your inner GPS. We know what is right in any circumstance within the deepest level of ourselves. Everyone has experienced his or her 'gut reaction' to some circumstance. In this world of bombardment by eternal stimuli it is a rare thing to take time to connect to our inner voice as a GPS to guide us in key decisions or actions. New age thinking has moved from being a subject of philosophy to that of science; physics to be exact.

The presence and power of our inner intelligence are now well understood. When you pay attention to that small voice within, you will experience improved decision-making. The resulting peace of mind you enjoy will expand for both yourself and those around you. If you feel doubt associated with your instinct it is wise to step back and reconsider. The 'right' action will feel positive, exciting, like a 'Yes'. It leaves you ready to move in an upward motion to something greater. It will never feel negative or like an unanswered question like 'Maybe' or 'Should I?' Trust yourself—you will know the right action to take when you take time to connect to and trust your inner intuition.

YOUR QUESTION THIS WEEK: How can you set aside 3 minutes in the morning and in the evening to sit in silence, allowing yourself to ask a question and get to know your inner GPS?

YOUR ACTION STEP: Before each key decision or action, create 3 minutes to go somewhere quiet to ask yourself if the step you are taking is the right one at this time. You will learn to 'hear' and 'feel' the GPS guidance of your intuition.

Example: When I sit quietly with a question like, 'Do I complete these meeting notes or scan the email for urgent messages?' 'Do I pay this bill or that bill?' 'Will I think about this now, tonight or tackle it in the morning?' or 'what would be the best outcome I can see for this situation?

> *"Trust yourself. You know more than you think you do." —Benjamin Spock*

WEEK 4: INVEST IN YOURSELF

"If we did the things we are capable of, we would astound ourselves." —Thomas Alva Edison

Each day we we consciously and unconsciously determine what we will invest our time in. According to research, about 95% of our day is spent on "autopilot" (just doing what is familiar) so we are not wide awake, engaged and conscious. We open our computer, assess our calendar, check our to-do lists and scan email for new priorities that may be rising to the surface. For the most part we are used to this daily routine and get annoyed with disruption. But, where is the aliveness? Where is the joyful investment for you to fulfill your vision for your life? Always choose aliveness.

You will spend your time doing something each day. The only question is, will you invest your time each day according to your own design, in alignment with your vision? Or, will you allow routine to take over, creating a life by default? We are capable of accomplishing anything we choose through the investment of our energy and focus. The day will pass, whether by design or by default. Make sure you are working each day to move in the direction of your life's vision.

YOUR QUESTION THIS WEEK: What can you do for 5 minutes each day to live inside your vision and to create a positive emotional state that will support your decisions as a leader?

Examples: Consider the sensory experience of already living in the successful outcome of your vision. You may be a philanthropist handing one of those four-foot cheque placards to your favourite charity; can you hear the audience applause? If you see yourself as leader of a global company, speaking to your Board, can you see the multiple video monitors projecting from around the world, feeling the shared excitement over your quarterly profits; a successful sales executive traveling and working with a level of high energy, all flights connecting with ease and clients happy with your product, service and personal integrity. Or perhaps you are walking across the stage in cap and gown receiving your graduate degree; do you see the bright stage lights as you shake hands with the Dean?

YOUR ACTION STEP: Schedule 5 minutes every day this week to invest in an activity that will move you toward your mission, vision or purpose. Create a poster or Pinterest page with pictures that bring your vision to life and spend 5 minutes looking at it each day. Time thieves will try to slip into your schedule, but stand guard. Consider these 5 minutes sacred to who you are becoming.

Example: Three years ago I envisioned what it would be like to be a successful author and professional speaker and spent 10 minutes each day seeing myself in front of a large audience, having a specified balance in my bank account at the end of the month, my bills paid in full and meeting my readers at book signing events. By investing time and energy into what I envisioned, it is a reality for me today.

> *"The energy of the mind is the essence of life."*
> *—Aristotle*

WEEK 5: CHOICE

"Between stimulus and response is a space. In this space lie our growth and our happiness."
—Unknown source; Stephen R. Covey, Daily Reflections for Highly Effective People

In the space described by Covey lies our ability to make a choice for ourselves. There are no right or wrong choices in life. There are simply choices. It's what you do with each choice, day in and day out, that will lead to a life of continuous learning, personal or professional growth and ultimately a clarification and fulfillment of the life you will love living as a leader. It is within each of us to move our life in the direction of our dreams by the choices we make and the actions we take. You have made a choice to be a leader. Choose what will lead you to an outcome you would love.

Each day I check in with myself to establish my mindset to make the best choices during my work day. I choose happiness; I choose to look for ways to support someone else to succeed; I choose to stay conscious enough of the current moment to forgive myself for my impatience during the day, remembering that we are all on a path in life that has bumps and challenges along the way. The most important choice I make is to be a person who benefits others in some way.

YOUR QUESTION THIS WEEK: How can I empower myself and others through the choices I make today? Example: I once considered leaving a job because I didn't feel recognized for my commitment, skills and talents. But in that moment of choice, instead of leaving, I chose to change my own mindset about my experience at work. I began to take an educational approach with both myself and those around me. As a result, rather than focusing on things that drew out criticism or complaint against others, I chose to focus on an internal state of satisfaction by recognizing how much knowledge and experience I had to offer. What I noticed in return was that the people I freely offered my experience to responded in kind and with appreciation and, important to me, recognition.

YOUR ACTION STEP: Don't wait for the title of 'leader' to act like one. You may want to choose to volunteer for a project or task team where results will make things easier, more efficient or empowering for your coworkers. Share your knowledge and experience freely and positively. Your daily choices reinforce your own satisfaction and meet your own needs as a leaders. Choose positivity, contribution and supportiveness.

"There are two primary choices in life: to accept conditions, as they exist or to accept the responsibility for changing them." —Denis Waitley

WEEK 6: TAKE ACTION

"The world is a dangerous place, not because of those who do evil, but because of those who look on and do nothing." —Albert Einstein

When we have a vision for our lives, we see that it is right for us to step in and step up. It has been said that there are three types of people in the world:

- Those that make things happen

- Those that watch what happens and

- Those that wonder what the heck just happened.

Envision the look on the faces of the people that believe in and support your decision to lead and maybe even those who doubt you. Feel how proud you are that you expressed your courage to follow through on your conviction to be a leader. Regardless of who on the team is chosen to champion a cause, as a leader your job is to ensure that your name is on the list of key participants.

> Be a positive 'activist' looking for solutions to workplace challenges.

During a phase in my life when I was at my most unhappy, I tried to withdraw from leadership by doing task-based activity each day. I would see a way to improve a circumstance for another person or for the organization overall and would think 'Someone else will figure it out' or worse, 'How can't they see the possible solution I see?' only to lay awake at night still thinking about what I knew and hadn't act upon. What I'd really done was given away my own power; hoarding my ability to create a better experience for myself and others was harmful to my own well being. From that experience, I discovered that you must own who you are as a leader. I understood two things: 1) how important it is to openly share your best thinking in any circumstance and 2) that when we are granted the insight to see how leading through action can increase engagement, satisfaction and reward for ourself and for others, we must act.

YOUR QUESTION THIS WEEK: Are you willing to take action when you see a need? What can you do that would aid your own learning or improve a situation for your coworkers?

Example: Address a system flaw for which you see a fix or improvement; open a dialogue with a colleague who you see running toward a politically risky situation; be a positive 'activist' looking for solutions to workplace challenges.

YOUR ACTION STEP: Reflect on an occasion where you saw a solution and did not take action based on the belief that someone else would 'do it' to 'figure it out'. Consider the opportunity that was presented to you that you passed up.'

Now, write out the following forgiveness statement for yourself: I forgive myself and release the feelings of self judgement I attach to my lack of action related to (state the circumstance). I commit to moving forward in life in a way that expresses my highest self through positive action.

Read your written statement to yourself every day this week and you will begin to feel a lightness in your self where that small weight once was.

You've taken action in two ways this week, one action in your role as a leader and one action for your own wellbeing.

"'I must do something' always solves more problems than 'Something must be done'."
—Author Unknown

WEEK 7: OPPORTUNITY

"When written in Chinese the word "crisis" is composed of two characters—one represents danger and the other represents opportunity."
—John F. Kennedy

As leaders, we are constantly looking for opportunities. We seek to understand the risks that lie within, but focus our attention, our energy and our thoughts on the possible opportunities in front of us. If we choose to ignore the gift of an opportunity within our sight by thinking it may require more of us, more work or more time, then we choose to ignore the greater possibilities that the opportunity may bring.

Opportunities unfold when there is an energetic alignment between our actions and our vision. Most often, opportunities show up like 'light bulb' ideas popping into our minds. As a leader you will find yourself carrying ideas forward just waiting for alignment with an opportunity. My experience has shown that if I don't stop to capture the idea, it can slip away, no longer clearly recalled many hours later. It takes practice to notice opportunities and to stop the clock in the moment to jot them down somewhere before moving on with your day.

YOUR QUESTION FOR THE WEEK: Have you noticed and ignored an opportunity in the last few weeks in the name of 'busy-ness'?

YOUR ACTION STEP: Write down a potential opportunity that you chose to ignore in the past week or one that arises in the week ahead. Annotate two things that you can do to bring this opportunity into the realm of possibility once again.

You could create the means to re-open a discussion in order to gain support to act on the opportunity you see.

Examples: Whether an empty parking space that I've driven past, or the ceation of a 30 minute 'think tank' time in my schedule, or an organizational redesign providing better alignment with the skills of the employees, I have always moved fast to capture the opportunity. I never let an opportunity slip by without an action, no matter how small.

"Ideas are like small fish, if they are not gaffed at the end of a pen, they quickly swim away, never to be seen again." —Anonymous

Chapter 2:
Listen and Learn

WEEK 8: LISTEN

"Learn all you can from the mistakes of others. You won't have time to make them all yourself." — Alfred Sheinwold

L isten intently. You will be surprised at what you learn when you make the effort to listen to other leaders around you. We receive little instruction in life on the nuances of being a great listener. Because none of us comes into our leadership role with the breadth of experience that the person before us left with, use your power to listen and observe as an opportunity to prepare. Listen to what others say and whom they engage, consult or collaborate with and you will also begin to recognize or hear what they do not say. Listen closely to their logic behind decisions being made.

I learned this best when I begain to sit in the same meeting rooms as the organization's most senior leaders. By watching and listening, I was able to more clearly see how the trust relationships between the individuals influenced the support for decisions being made. There were numerous occasions where I witnessed a leader change their position on an issue based on great listening skills, i.e., listening to understand.

Actively listening to learn removes the disconnect that can result from selective hearing and is a short cut to greater success sooner.

YOUR QUESTION THIS WEEK: Do you listen with the intent to hear the message conveyed and perhaps learn how to integrate a demonstrated skill and technique into your own toolkit? Observe your own listening behaviour. Do you listen to understand and learn or are you busy formulating your answer to jump in with a response to what is being said before the other person's statement is completed?

Examples: We can pick up an attitude, pick up the engagement language, or pick up techniques like how to keep a meeting moving toward answers and solutions instead of worry and complaint.

YOUR ACTION STEP: This week do less talking and more listening to others around you, with the specific intention of learning successful ways of 'being' a leader.

"Two monologues do not make a dialogue."
—Jeff Daly

WEEK 9: THE GIFT OF THE NEGATIVE

"Your most unhappy customers are your greatest source of learning." —Bill Gates, 'Business @ the Speed of Thought'

When you receive complaints about your service you receive a great gift as a leader.

A complaint is a flag raised to indicate that you are unaware of an unintended consequence of an action taken or not taken. Consider a complaint a 'heads up' that will move you into action. When an action or a design for your process is flawed in a way that you haven't foreseen, there is fertile ground for complaint. A leader isn't 'bothered' by complaints, a leader is grateful for receiving the complaint as feedback in order to move into discovery and solution design that will meet their customer or employee's needs more effectively.

Example: I spent years in hospital record departments listening to physicians complain about the constrictive circumstances in which they were forced to complete their patient documentation. That is, until I asked myself this question—'What can I do to be a person who seeks to improve the circumstance for others?' What emerged was an opportunity for dialogue built on open exchange and supportive intention. This mindset increased the number of calls from my 'customers' (they initiate contact and engagement) and increased my ability to create improvements in both processes and relationships.

YOUR QUESTION THIS WEEK: When you receive a complaint, is your first reaction that of Winnie the Pooh, 'Oh, bother' or one of gratitude?

YOUR ACTION STEP: Talk with your team this week about the gratitude mindset when receiving compaints and then talk together about what would be an approach to take to improve the support you provide to your customers and staff.

Example: I once worked with a group of staff to develop a common script to use when answering the telephone. Instead of 'Hello, this is the xyz department', we posed a question to the caller, 'Hello, you've reached xyz department. How can I help you?'. This took the edge off even the crustiest caller and reinforced our own gratitude that we could be present for the caller and be empowered to be of service. Those complaints very quickly turned to compliments.

"We often refuse to accept an idea merely because the tone of voice in which it has been expressed is unsympathetic to us." —Friedrich Nietzsche

WEEK 10: FEEDBACK

"Criticism may not be agreeable, but it is necessary. It fulfills the same function as pain in the human body. It calls attention to an unhealthy state of things." —Winston Churchill

Although praise is an important expression of gratitude for others and their work, feedback is an important part of the growth cycle for us. We all receive feedback every day and, because we sometimes perceive it as negative, we need practice at receiving it with a mindset that opens the gift hidden within it. We often receive feedback when it is needed to get our attention and to wake us up. Maybe we have acted in a way that has not met defined expectations, not met our personal commitments or not taken notice of the needs of others. Next time feedback comes your way, welcome it, look for the value of the wakeup call and use it to find a new perspective by asking yourself what is the message behind it. This isn't easy, nor is it comfortable, but it is important to our personal growth as leaders. The ability to receive feedback is a measurement of emotional maturity.

Once I learned to hear, receive and respond to feedback with enough balance in my own perspective to not fully engage at a purely emotional level, I was able to speed my entry into learning what the feedback had to offer. The need to step back and release the emotional response I do feel continues to sometimes catch me off guard, but with practice, the frequency and duration of the emtional response has lessened.

Don't mistake the release of an emotional response with detachment. We cannot detach or 'shrug off' the negative feeback and expect to learn and improve from it. We must own it and act on it in order to strengthen ourselves as leaders.

Watch for feedback. It's everywhere, reflecting to you the very opportunites you need for growth as a leader.

QUESTION THIS WEEK: Has something you've done attracted feedback from others?

YOUR ACTION STEPS: Think about the last time you received negative feedback for something you had or had not done.

1. Reflect on the feelings of that moment and release feelings like hurt or embarrassment in order to receive the value that resides in the feedback received.

    Example: Feedback you may receive in a day isn't always in the form of words. It can look like body language, facial expressions, tone of voice, participation of others or lack thereof.

2. Write down what you can learn from the feedback received from others.

"The final proof of greatness lies in being able to endure criticism without resentment." —Elbert Hubbard

WEEK 11: STRESS

"Learn wisdom from the ways of a seedling. A seedling, which is never hardened off through stressful situations, will never become a strong productive plant." —Stephen Sigmund

We sometimes allow 'stressful situations' to be an excuse not to step into leadership. Stress just means we are out of our comfort zone and we have an opportunity to grow! And, stressful circumstances can be positive or negative. Leaders work on mastering our response to the stressors we experience.

Stress at work is no different than the stress that exists in every other area of life whether it is health, relationships, time or money.

Let's look at stress as an example of polarity. The universe we live in consists of magnetic energy; a universe of polarity. As a leader, there will be days that you will feel the negative pull more strongly and it will take more effort and more energy to create balance with it by using a positive thought, positive approaches or positive actions. Every thought molecule has a positive and negative charge and, as leaders, it is our privilege to enter the thought molecule and wrestle for the side of the positive charge.

> Stress just means we are out of our comfort zone and we have an opportunity to grow.

When we are feeling 'over stressed' it is related to our inability to reinstate the balance of the polarity in the circumstance based on our experience or state of belief we are in. The same experience can occur with positive stressors. We can certainly feel that we are out of our comfort zone or out of balance when we perceive that we are the recipients of 'too much of a good thing'. Have you ever said, 'This can't really be happening—pinch me'? We can feel stress associated with positive circumstances as well as negative.

QUESTION THIS WEEK: Let's focus on the perception of negative stress. When you find yourself at the negative pole of a thought or action do you consciously put effort into pulling yourself to a postion of balance with positive thoughts? Or do you choose to allow the negative pull to mount its strength against you?

YOUR ACTION STEP: This week, strengthen your ability to reinstate balance into every thought and circumstance by finding an opportunity for personal growth hidden within.

Use a scratch pad to keep a tally of the number of times you catch yourself in a negative thought—you'll be surprised at how frequent the opportunities to decrease small stressors come your way. Do the tally daily and it will build your consciousness around the tug of negativity for which you must move into positive thought and action in order to maintain your positive balance. Along the way, I have learned about the things that trigger a reactive response within me, allowing me to experience the stress reaction less frequently.

Example: This act has provided me with a positive reinforcement process. I recall that my early 'tallies' were in multiples of

10's , now my tally of obvious negative thoughts is fewer than 5 most days. I am now able to catch myself, replaced the negative thought with a positive one and benefit by reducing unhealthy stress.

"There must be a positive and negative in everything in the universe in order to complete a circuit or circle, without which there would be no activity, no motion." —John McDonald

WEEK 12: NO EASY ANSWER

Dilemma: A situation that requires one to choose between two equally balanced alternatives; a predicament that defies a satisfactory solution. (Dictionary definition)

Sometimes there is no clear-cut, right/wrong decision to make. In many cases there are competing issues at hand where many options can serve the need. It is right to create job security but it is also right to maintain budgetary control during inflationary cost increases. It is right to spend time improving the quality of your work but it is also right to meet deadlines and avoid 'diminishing returns' of the effort required for near perfection. When you are faced with a difficult choice, you will need to ensure that any conflicting views have been voiced. Look at your decision in light of organizational values, policy and a balance of fairness. Know that these decisions are not going to result in 100% of the people being happy. As a leader you must have the discipline to ensure an ethical and balanced approach is taken to reach your decision, a decision you can easily defend if asked to.

I was about 10 years into my career when I first realized the value of a mentor. The idea that I did not have to be the Lone Ranger in my decision-making was enlightening and the perceived weight of my decision-making responsibilities lifted from my shoulders. To be able to talk through your decision- making process is important to both you and the recipients of your decision. To be able to talk through your decision-making process with a trusted colleague is invaluable to your success and to your career.

YOUR QUESTION THIS WEEK: Has a decision you need to make have you wishing you could delay or ignore it?

Examples: Will you address or ignore someone's disrespectful behavior? Will you work on the meeting preparation tonight or tomorrow? Will I spend the budget money on equipment or team recognition?

YOUR ACTION STEP: It may be helpful to have a trusted colleague or a leader you respect assist you with your dilemma this week. Begin your personal search for a mentor who can remain neutral while you talk out the decision making process and determine a decision you can confidently defend.

"We can try to avoid making choices by doing nothing, but even that is a decision." —Gary Collins

WEEK 13: WORRY

"I've developed a new philosophy... I only dread one day at a time." —Charlie Brown (Charles Schulz)

Don't worry about what happened yesterday. It is behind you. Today, the only thing you need to do is take action to address the gaps that were discovered yesterday but which you were unable to address in real time.

Don't ruin your day today by worrying about what might happen tomorrow. If you are prepared for an expected event tomorrow there is nothing in existence today for you to actually worry about. Beyond what you know are likely risks to prepare for, there are endless circumstances that could come into play based on the interactions of dozens of other people connected to you and their related circumstances. We cannot control the future any more than we can control the weather, but we can manage it in a positive way when it arrives by taking positive action in the moment. Consider what you are worrying about that may never happen. Wait for it to play into the active state of 'today' before you use your time and energy to resolve a problem that may or may not arise.

Perhaps the worst type of worry is a worry that you share with your team. What happens? Well, in a team of 10 people, you now have 10 people thinking there must be something they should be worrying about and the energy of worry and uncertainty erodes the productive work of the day.

YOUR QUESTION THIS WEEK: Do you notice that you feel worry or anxiety on a regular basis? Do you worry about outcomes that are still unknown, might happen but, then again, might not? Have you shared your worries with your team?

YOUR ACTION STEP: Pay attention to your feelings of worry this week. Do they arise related to issues of yesterday (follow up action), today (action) or the future (unknown action)? Write down any worries that you have about the future and notice that without certainty, which only exists in the current moment, there is nothing you can act upon. So, observe and wait. Your worries will evaporate. And once the reality of tomorrow becomes today, you will have a clear view of what you are facing.

"I am an old man. I have known a great many troubles, most of them never happened." —Mark Twain

WEEK 14: VALUE

"Try not to become a man of success, but rather try to become a man of value." —Albert Einstein

Since the very early years of my career, I have done my best to bring something of value to both the task at hand and the organization overall. As you become proficient in applying your listening and creativity with your desire to lead, ideas and opportunities will pop up all around you. Watch for the ideas and opportunities that will bring financial value, service value or system value to your business. Of course, it's not enough to only notice ideas, you must act.

With this mindset, I've been able to not only keep myself challenged but have created almost every job I've ever held based on opportunities I have seen where I could add value. The knowledge and skill I have obtained have supported me by ever increasing my value to others. And, of note, the value you bring will almost always show up in relationship to the salary you attract.

QUESTION THIS WEEK: What ideas do you have for adding value to the organization that you haven't yet shared with others?

Examples: An idea can be related to anything, such as changing job responsibilities for better alignment with your or someone else's strengths and skills; altering scheduled work shifts to have more people available in the early evening when customers have returned home at the end of the day; establishing a network of subject matter experts that can be sourced by anyone in the company.

YOUR ACTION STEP: Review your ideas and define how you could target your work effort on delivering value. What is one step you can take to bring value to your workplace this week? Perhaps there's a need that is not currently being filled?

"You don't get paid for the hour. You get paid for the value you bring to the hour." —Jim Rohn

Chapter 3:
Energize Yourself and Others

"If you think you can, you can. And if you think you can't, you're right." —Henry Ford

When we have difficulty believing we can accomplish what we set out to do, it is helpful to create a vision of the new you, an avatar of sorts that is the new you, the you that you intend to become. Your new, successful self feels strong, confident and capable. When an old story starts to play in your head around 'I can't do that' or 'who am I to think I could?' or 'I'm not good enough to deserve that', hit the "Pause Button" and say to yourself, 'Stop! Of course I can'. You are not that previous version of yourself anymore. Every day is new. Act as if you are already the next version of you. You are capable of doing anything you set your mind to, anything you believe in. We don't attract what we want, we attract WHO WE ARE and it's all based on our self-perception. Of course you can. You ARE that new version of yourself. You have simply been waiting to emerge.

> You are capable of doing anything you set your mind to, anything you believe in.

Over the years, science has caught up with the application and power of the mind-body connection. Understanding the relationship of my thoughts to my outcomes has shown up in many ways, in real estate transactions, in the work I have created, in my relationships, in becoming an author. But the most powerful, has been my level of confidence that I can be, and do, and accomplish whatever I desire.

When I was first called upon to take on the responsibility to be the 'Manager' of a department, I hadn't been a manager before and I didn't know all the responsibilities of or skills required by a manager. But I created the vision of what my best manager self would be. First I created the external version of the new me —business suit, briefcase, sitting in an office with a window, a door and a small table in the corner of the space where I could meet with an employee who may want to talk with me in private. Then, I thought about how I would feel in that role—proud to be given the honor of this new challenge, respected by peer managers, satisfied by my ability to meet the challenges of budgets, staffing, planning and happy to be recognized by my peers as capable in this role. I adopted and used the phrase "I can do that" every time someone asked me to do something or every time I volunteered to take something on, reinforcing my avatar's belief that 'I could'. And guess what. I did.

Find confidence in the knowing that every person is born with everything they need to accomplish their goals and dreams. Believe in yourself.

YOUR QUESTION THIS WEEK: Do you find yourself in your 'old story' using words like 'I can't . . .'? 'I'm not . . .', 'and I'll never be . . .'?

YOUR ACTION STEP: When you think you can't, stop yourself (hit the "Pause Button") and go back into the feeling that you are a successful person deserving each success that will come your way. Live from your avatar every day this week.

Example: Embody your avatar by stating, 'I am the woman/man who . . .' and soon you will see that it is just as easy to believe in the 'I can' as it once was to believe in the I 'can't'.

"Don't wait until everything is just right. It will never be perfect. There will always be challenges, obstacles and less than perfect conditions. So what. Get started now. With each step you take, you will grow stronger and stronger, more and more skilled, more and more self-confident and more and more successful." —Mark Victor Hansen

WEEK 16: TAKE ACTION

"Great talent finds happiness in execution." —Goethe

A strong leader is the one who has the sense to surround himself with winning people. Leaders are winners and winners are people that find pleasure in action. Each one of us wakes up in the morning wanting to know that what we do produces value in our life and in the lives of others. Through our actions as leaders we support others to understand how their own actions lead to the success of the team, the organization and themselves. Allow for learning through action.

YOUR QUESTION THIS WEEK: How can you provide your team with opportunities to think outside of the box and the confidence to take "imperfect action" that would move them closer to the goal?

Whether you read this chapter and think about building your career, the success of your team, or your personal relationships, it is beneficial to know that perfection has for centuries been reserved for The Infinite for a reason. Nothing in our world is perfect, and waiting for the perfect state, the perfect time or the perfect place, will do nothing but produce waiting. Without action there is nothing for you to build upon. Life is an iterative process; we are constantly changing. And for those of you who have been a 'high achiever' throughout your life, you will likely take longer to embrace this notion of acting without perfection, slowing the cycle of change in your own perceptions. But the beauty of letting go of perfection lies in the peace of mind, unexpected joy and improved relationships with others that you will experience once you do.

YOUR ACTION STEP: Encourage people to take imperfect action and to see the value of their own contributions to the organization by allowing them to move the team toward the goal.

Example: When I learned that everyone likes to be involved in the work at hand in some way, I realized that I didn't have to be the one and only to create, write and present the perfect Committee Terms of Reference or the perfect procedure. I had to let go of the fear that I would be judged as less competent because of incomplete/imperfect work and just get something out there as a target for people to shoot at. By inviting others to add and edit any document I wrote, I not only learned how to engage others but I reduced the self induced pressure to get something done 'right' before I let it see the light of day. I could get assistance, receive the best ideas of the collective group and have people feel like they were part of the creation. Learning to allow others to see my incomplete effort has resulted in more great work getting completed through collaboration and has taught me the win-win of taking action.

"It is common sense to take a method and try it. If it fails, admit it frankly and try another. But above all, try something." —Franklin D. Roosevelt

WEEK 17: DO IT!

"Knowing is not enough; we must apply!" —Goethe

We learn best by doing. Because we all have more things to do than time with which to do them, we must be focused on doing what's most needed. Be careful not to do what is the easiest or the task with the least resistance unless its completion directly serves your goal.

Example: Although this is 'dating' me, I'm sure I'm not alone when I share the story of a day when email was becoming the most commonly used communication tool in the workplace. I was excited to be able to make the instant connection of my message with the intended receiver efficiently, doing more each day than ever before. One day, the Chief Medical Officer for our organization called and asked to see me. He asked me to make a very simple change in the way I was taking action, "Please stop emailing the medical staff. They just want you to use the phone." This could be a story about communication, and it is in many ways, but in this context, I want to share with you that taking action needs to be done in a way that suits the context. My efficiency gained by prioritizing the use of email did not support the most important goal of the organization, which was personal engagement.

YOUR QUESTION THIS WEEK: Are you tempted to take action based solely on ease?

YOUR ACTION STEP: This week watch how you prioritize the use of your time so that you get the important things done, especially when they are not the easiest items on your 'to do' list. Let your goals guide you.

The steps to take, with an example using my story above, include:

1. Establish clarity on what result you are required to achieve, e.g. personal engagement

2. Prioritize your activities in relationship to the value they will bring in serving your primary goal or your customer, e.g. phone call, then email

3. Make the decision to tackle one item that will make the greatest contribution, regardless of how difficult it may appear, e.g. make the calls you think may be the most difficult first

4. List the series of actions needed to reach completion, e.g., build the contact list

5. Take action! e.g., make the calls

Start this morning with your new prioritization criteria and ask yourself, "What actions today will deliver the greatest contribution to those I serve?"

"There is nothing so useless as doing efficiently that which should not be done at all." —Peter Drucker

Week 18: Accountability

"When life gives you lemons, please, just don't squirt them in other people's eyes." —J. Andrew Helt

When things go wrong, we might believe it is best for all involved to place blame squarely onto someone, but the truth is there is value in welcoming accountability to rest with you yourself. A leader knows that accountability can rest on the shoulders of the team. From the first person to the last person in the chain of events, there is something that someone could have done differently to create a different outcome. Identifying the missteps of others is easier than seeing our own. The secret to growing from what may seem like a 'burden' of accountability is to understand that as soon as you accept yourself as being accountable, you open the opportunity to review and learn by connecting the dots that will prevent the same thing from happening again.

Holding yourself accountable also provides you with the opportunity to teach others about the dots connected so they are able to intervene earlier in the process before there's a 'next' time. Give yourself and others the gift of being the individual who can prevent repeated or similar negative results in the future. Become a solution expert that connects the dots for others.

Example: This lesson was most powerfully demonstrated for me with my work in technology implementation projects. There is always something unexpected that occurs. We were implementing a new system for registering patients coming into the hospital for treatment. Part of this process is entering all prior and current patients into the computer system. During the 1st week we began to receive feedback that our census counts were off for some nursing units. This was an opportunity for finger pointing. Was it the hospital registration clerks, the IT department, the nursing units? Working backward to determine the root cause, it turned out that on the day of 'go-live', every patient going out the door was not entered from paper into the system as 'discharged'. We got them all into the system as planned, but on that one very busy day, we missed getting them signed out of the system. The discharge process touched all three departments with no single area or person at fault. What we learned together was that without assigning blame, we were focused on finding the cause of the problem and the creation of the solution that we were all a part of.

YOUR QUESTION THIS WEEK: Is there a negative outcome that you have recently been tempted to 'blame' someone else for? When you retrace your steps starting at the outcome, where were you in the sequence? On reflection, was there an opportunity for you to jump in with a communication, a question, or an action that could have altered the outcome?

YOUR ACTION STEP: This week, make a conscious choice to address issues by owning them. Then take time to identify and connect the dots with others involved without attaching blame.

Example: Draw out the steps you have already tracked back through in your own mind; ask the team to review and insert any other steps they are aware of. I like to use Post-It® notes for this work as you insert steps and move the pieces to fit the actual activities that took place; collectively you will be able to find the weak links where an error may have occurred.

This empowers everyone to learn to recognize potential risks and be accountable for building better outcomes in the future.

"We are too busy mopping the floor to turn off the faucet." —Author Unknown

WEEK 19: ATTITUDES

"Attitudes are contagious. Are yours worth catching?" —Dennis and Wendy Mannering

Each day you wake up with the gift to decide how you will 'be' for the day. You are always at a point of choice. Understanding how a bad attitude can affect everyone, you don't want to be the one to dampen everyone else's energy, enthusiasm and creativity. Choose to 'be' the one who sees the glass half full, or better yet, overflowing. Choose to 'be' the one who finds the good to be harvested from every circumstance. Choose to 'be' the person who lightens the atmosphere with an understanding that each of us chooses our attitude for the day. A positive person will stay productive, motivated and moving in the direction of success. As a leader, you set an example to others with a positive attitude.

Example: I am very sensitive to my surroundings, impacted by both people and my environment. Factors like lighting, heat and noise are things that often have a greater influence on me than others and my positive attitude can quickly fall into a negative mood. There are days when I am fully challenged by life in a cubicle farm and I find myself grumpy with everything and everyone around me. I need to take notice, make an adjustment to my attitude and turn it around as quickly as possible. I know I impact others around me.

When we let the external circumstances in our day get to us, we can negatively impact everyone around us. Eleanor Roosevelt once stated, "All the water in the world won't hurt you unless you let it inside".

YOUR QUESTION THIS WEEK: How often do you catch yourself holding onto a negative or cranky attitude during your day? How does holding onto that attitude impact you and others around you?

YOUR ACTION STEPS: Pull yourself out of a 'bad' attitude as soon as you notice yourself being negative by using the steps below.

1. Notice—Notice that your attitude demonstrated through communications received or delivered and through your personal interactions with others. Actively notice this as it occurs.

2. Hit 'Pause'—Consciously hit the 'Pause' button. Stop yourself from continuing to act from that negative mindset.

3. Redirect—Tell yourself to switch it up and adjust your attitude to one of optimism.

Look for opportunities to bring out your positive attitude in every circumstance or interaction you have.

> *"Attitudes are nothing more than habits of thoughts, and habits can be acquired. An action repeated becomes an attitude realized." —Paul Myer*

WEEK 20: PERSONAL MOTIVATION

"I don't like that man. I must get to know him better." —Abraham Lincoln

Remain silent until you understand the motivation of others. Being critical or exclusive will not serve your purpose and simply wastes the time and energy you could be applying to something that moves your interests forward. If you take the time to understand what all parties need from any situation or outcome, what their personal interest is in participating, you will meet your own needs as well as theirs. Make the effort to ask questions that will give you insight into how others perceive a shared situation. The truth is that every one of us sees the same thing differently based on our own knowledge, experience, values and beliefs. You will increase the group's awareness of the many paths leading to the same result. Become more aligned through gaining understanding of what each group member wants from the experience and results will be achieved sooner.

> Take time to understand what all parties need from any situation.

Example: I am currently working with a committee to improve policy governance and process across the organization. Members represent over 20 departments so it makes sense that as individuals we are looking for different outcomes, some focused on speed and efficiency, some on front-line staff engagement and some to fill in the policy gaps we see creating confusion for our operational teams. Knowing the multitude of outcomes desired, we will be more likely to create the collective support and compliance needed with whatever our result because we have taken time to establish an understanding of one another's needs.

YOUR QUESTION THIS WEEK: Have you rushed into a new group assignment or committee meeting without taking the time to understand who the other members are, what their goals are and what they see as their benefit from participating?

YOUR ACTION STEP: Introduce the relevant information about you and your motivation to the other members of a group you are working with, even if the group has already been established and work is underway. Encourage each of them to provide the same insight to the others.

Example: A tool I picked up recently, that originated in NESTA, a British Innovation organization, is the 'Randomized Coffee Trial'. If you've heard of a randomized control drug trial in health research you'll see the relationship to this process immediately. If not, let me describe it. With a group of people from diverse roles and different departments, put the names in a hat and pull names to set up pairs (the random selection). The two individuals who have been matched will meet in person or online for a 30 minute coffee conversation. The Randomized Coffee Trial is a great team builder for highly functioning and communicative group work. Our sessions were guided with an outline of introductions, a 'who-am-I' background description with an exchange of inquiry to understand the other person's story followed by the sharing of thoughts on questions related to what is expected from our participation on the Committee. You'll want to talk fast. Be ready to be surprised at what you learn and what you have in common with your coffee partner as well as the interesting and often winding paths that make a career. I guarantee that your time will run out before your subject matter does.

"Sometimes the path you're on is not as important as the direction you're heading." —Kevin Smith

WEEK 21: CONTRIBUTION

"I never see what has been done; I only see what remains to be done." —Marie Curie

There is a principle in physics established by Aristotle and supported by physicists like Newton and Einstein called 'Horror vacui', that is, 'Nature hates a vacuum'. This principle eloquently explains the law that predicts that no space will be left unfilled in the universe. To take a lighter approach to the fact that substance always rushes in to fill any void we see this every day in our work. As the work continues to flow in and pile up around us it is challenging but critical to purposely stop and appreciate our accomplishments.

Example: To my regret, there have been years in my career where I haven't taken the time to even acknowledge what my major accomplishments have been. This inattention to my accomplishments doesn't just leave me scratching my head in creating a resume, but likely undermined my ability to approach new work with the freshness and enthusiasm it deserved.

We will never suffer from a shortage of work to do, but what we often suffer from is a failure to recognize our own contribution to the betterment of all that is in our sphere of influence.

YOUR QUESTION THIS WEEK: Do you take time to reflect and give yourself recognition for a task completed before you jump into the next?

YOUR ACTION STEP: Schedule 30 minutes for you to document the projects or assignments that you have participated in and/or completed in the past six months. Remember to demonstrate an appreciation for all we have been honored to bring to our life in the workplace. Fill the space left by task completion with a few moments of recognition and gratitude for your accomplishment.

Example: A walk back through your calendar can help your memory. Amazing how much you contribute in this world, isn't it?

"Out of the strain of the doing, into the peace of the done." —Julia Woodruff, Gone

WEEK 22: TRUTH

"Beware of the half-truth. You may have gotten hold of the wrong half." —Author Unknown

Become your own fact checker. When you hear 'the latest news,' don't just be certain of your source but be certain of their source as well. There is a seed of truth in every rumor and there is someone's truth in every statement made. You don't want to be repeating something that is later proven unsubstantiated or downright incorrect. Most often, a simple phone call or email can clarify what you are hearing and what the original message and intent was. This allows you to restate the facts with your own interpretation and voice without having diluted or changed the message through other people's filters. This will build your own trustworthiness in the eyes of others.

YOUR QUESTION THIS WEEK: Have you ever been considered an unreliable source because information you repeated from a third party was incorrect? Reflect on why you chose to repeat it without checking the facts.

Examples: You wanted to believe the statement; you trusted the individual would have checked the facts; you have been waiting for some information on the same subject and thought 'this must be it' without confirming.

YOUR ACTION STEP: This week, as you listen to colleagues giving 'the latest update', take time to check the facts before you repeat any information received from someone other than the source.

Example: Pick up the phone and ask what the individual can tell you about a specified situation. This way you can hear the story first hand, complete with voice intonation, hesitancy or commitment to what is being said.

"Do not repeat anything you will not sign your name to." —Author Unknown

WEEK 23: TEAMWORK

"Individual commitment to a group effort—that is what makes teamwork, a company work, a society work, a civilization work." —*Vince Lombardi*

Some of us have a more natural penchant for teamwork than others. For those of us who live much of our life in pursuits that involve only ourselves, we sometimes miss the value of working in a team. We think thoughts like "I could do it quicker myself." Although this may prove true in terms of the total time required to complete a task, it does not guarantee a better or best outcome.

We're all familiar with the idea that 'many hands make light work' or the synergistic effect of a group of people is greater than the sum of its parts. Here's another perspective.

When we come into a team we must be willing to offer our own knowledge, skills, experience and ideas but be equally willing to stay open to the learning from the multitude of ideas from others whose knowledge, skills and experience differ from our own. I believe this is where the real value in teamwork lies. The collective learning and solution development from the group experience and wisdom always outstrips the value of doing it 'quicker'.

YOUR QUESTION THIS WEEK: How many times do you find yourself thinking you should just 'do it' and move on to the next thing without having to discuss it with a group?

YOUR ACTION STEP: Each time you are brought into a team discussion or committee meeting this week, pay attention to the nuggets of new insight that come to you from what another team member has shared, and commit to actively sharing what you know or have experienced that is related to the current task. Learn to allow yourself to approach teamwork as both a 'teacher and learner', in addition to the common role as a member or 'doer'.

> *"Teamwork is the ability to work together toward a common vision. It's the ability to direct individual accomplishment toward organizational objectives. It is the fuel that allows common people to attain uncommon results." —Andrew Carnegie*

WEEK 24: SUPPORTING OTHERS

"Don't smother each other. No one can grow in the shade." —Leo Buscaglia

There are very few creations in this world that we can bring to life without the assistance of others. As a leader you are in a position to assist others in their development by asking for their participation in work projects. This is especially important for those who do not yet have the experience of planning or decision-making that you may already have. Don't let yourself hold people aside because they do not have the experience today. They will only gain experience through doing. Bring your team out of the background and into the meeting rooms to help them grow into their future selves as well. You will all gain if you support others as they learn through new opportunities to serve. Give opportunities to others so they can share the light.

> As a leader you are in a position to assist others in their development.

YOUR QUESTION THIS WEEK: Do you keep all the new and interesting activities to yourself?

Example: Do you find yourself not trusting the people around you to do the job at hand? Ask what it would take for you to be their support and mentor. What are you willing to give?

YOUR ACTION STEP: Write down one way that you can more fully support others to move forward with their career goals and work satisfaction by inviting them to represent you and the team at a meeting or committee meeting.

Example: Explain that you expect an update and ongoing engagement on the subject and let them know how you are willing to support them as they move forward in this new territory.

"The deed is everything, the glory naught."
—Johann Wolfgang von Goethe

WEEK 25: FAILURE

"'The horror of that moment,' the King went on, 'I shall never, never forget!' 'You will, though'. The Queen said, 'If you don't make a memorandum of it'." —Lewis Carroll, Through the Looking Glass, 1872

When we stumble in life, we tend to see our mistakes as failures and believe we have to be reminded of these regularly in order to pay some penalty for our error. The price we really need to pay is to taking the time to understand that the gift in mistakes is the learning we gain from them. Take the lesson and learn it well, allow the failure to convert to something you work on strengthening for yourself. The incident itself is in the past, there is nothing you can do to 'undo' what happened. Know that it's perfectly reasonable for you to move forward without carrying this with you like baggage. Let yourself forget these transgressions so that you have a lighter, more enthusiastic flight as you rise upward in your career.

I can give you a long list of life experiences that could be framed as failures if I chose to dwell on them in the negative. Each of you could make a list just as long—life is a learning experience. A friend of mine taught me to quickly let go of whatever current mistake I thought I made, whether in a personal relationship or at work, by saying "Yet another 'growth experience'." Yup, those 'growth experiences' can show up every week. It's done, move on. Tomorrow's another day. The truth in Lewis Carroll's King's quotation is that noone ever remembers the 'horrors' of your making but you, if you choose to. Everyone else moves on.

YOUR QUESTION THIS WEEK: How readily do you release a failure? Do you assign it enough weight that it has a mental memorandum dedicated to it, dragging it around like a lead weight attached to your mind and body?

YOUR ACTION STEP: Take a past failure you have in your memory. Understanding that you cannot undo it, find the lesson within the experience and convert it to a new strength, then release the incident itself. You can capitalize on the learning without hauling around the incident itself, forever replaying it in your mind.

One way you can approach this is to write out in your own language what you see as a point of failure in your performance. Then, write your part in that failure in first person, i.e. I did xyz. Now you can look at the language you've used to describe your action from that harsh finger-pointing voice and rewrite it as if it is a more gentle and compassionate message of feedback to your best friend about what you see didn't work. Treat failure as feedback. You simply won't handle the same challenge with the same response in the future. To close, identify what you've learned from that feedback and what remedies you may need to make for closure of the very worst of cases.

Or, you might just say 'Who cares!' and shake it off. And you'll be right—no one else will care as deeply as you do.

"Failure is only the opportunity to begin again more intelligently." —Henry Ford

Chapter 4:
Meeting Challenges

Week 26: Trouble Ahead

"If I had a formula for bypassing trouble, I would not pass it round. Trouble creates a capacity to handle it. I don't embrace trouble; that's as bad as treating it as an enemy. But I do say meet it as a friend, for you'll see a lot of it and had better be on speaking terms with it." —Oliver Wendell Holmes

A s we walk along the path of our career we are bound to face what we see as obstacles. These are simply things that are outside the library of our current experience. Every challenge we overcome opens our minds to greater thinking, new ideas, new paths to solutions. We expand our ability to face all things unexpected.

Challenges require you to maintain focus on the goal you will achieve. Using a combination of reflection and forward thinking to strategically address challenges keeps us on track to reach our goal. Focus on the goal and 'what' you want to create, rather than 'how' you will do it while you are brainstorming for a solution. The 'how' can be addressed once you have the right 'what' defined as your target stated.

You will always work with people who find it easier to think of a solution before fully understanding the problem and you and I are no different. We can be caught in the same search for rapid solution in the interest of time and the desire to 'fix' the problem. A quick solution can put out a fire, but a quick solution isn't always the effective and efficient solution. If I work from the front end, I will create a list of 'to do's, some may create resolution and some may not. If I take the time to focus on the end result I desire instead of the quick fix, the ideas for actions to take will differ. I like to think my way to action by looking at both sides of the original goal—particularly the far side of the goal, i.e. what might result from its achievement. This gives a different perspective to the current exercise of problem solving. Think your way backward from the goal before thinking from the current situation forward. It is a subtle change in approach but it activates our creative mind and brings additional options to mind.

Example: I misplaced my keys this week. Did I start searching based on the hundreds of locations they could be based on my life, i.e. kitchen, bathroom, garage, car, mailbox, suitcase, shoes, laundry room? No, this would not be efficient.

You know that the fastest way to success is to work backward. I had been thinking from my current state, unable to find my keys. I worked my way back from there, retracing my exact steps and actions of the morning. I retraced every place that matched with getting ready for work that morning but without any luck. By extending and reframing my search from the last time I had my keys in my hand, I moved from getting 'out' of the house to getting 'into' the house the night before. I opened the door, dropped my bag, slipped off my shoes and hung up my coat— voila—the keys were inside my coat pocket. Putting on a coat wasn't in my action sequence that morning, so I never went to the closet for a coat. Working backward uses the power of memory associated with every step taken during the course of a day.

YOUR QUESTION THIS WEEK: How often do you stray from the goal when you are distracted by something you didn't see coming? Do you then get caught up in the 'how' before you have determined the 'what' associated with the challenge?

YOUR ACTION STEP: Stay focused on the outcome you are intended to reach as you seek the 'what' to do when defining a solution for an arising challenge. Don't get so caught up in the minutia of the 'how' that you lose sight of the target state. Practice working backward as often as possible to activate your creative mind

"Smooth seas do not make skillful sailors."
—African Proverb

WEEK 27: PRIORITIES

"If you break your neck, if you have nothing to eat, if your house is on fire, then you got a problem. Everything else is inconvenience." —Robert Fulghum

Unless a life is at stake, we really don't need to put every one of our body's cells on high alert. Keep things in perspective.

Our people are important, our services are important, our business is important but it is only one piece in the great puzzle of life. Unless we work in a first responder profession, there is unlikely a chance that one of us will die if a problem is not brought to final resolution today. That is not to say that our lives tomorrow will not be easier if we resolve things today, but certainly no one will die if we don't.

I have worked with people who believe the sky will fall if a question isn't answered within minutes of it being posed. I guarantee you will work with these people too. My experience has shown me that making too high a priority of daily injections of questions, ideas or new initiatives will set the whole team on edge and dilute the focus of energy on current deliverables. Your team members are likely already fully engaged in what were priorities up until that moment. I can find myself consistently bumping tasks in my calendar to respond to the latest phone call, or reaction to someone's new idea. I stop the intensity of my own reaction (potential panic) by asking questions to determine exactly what is required, by when, for whom, to serve what purpose (why) and in what form is the response to take (how to deliver). If I do have to shift priorities, I will at least hit the target response more accurately than I would have by simply lighting everyone on fire to react like there's a life and death emergency.

YOUR QUESTION THIS WEEK: Do you ever find a lack of planning turns into deadlines that leave you feeling the pressure of a life-threatening emergency? How can you better plan your own goals and activities to ensure your deadlines are met without the last minute stress of urgency being placed on others?

YOUR ACTION STEP: Look at your upcoming deadlines. Go to your calendar and block time to do the work required in order for your deadline to be met through calm, focused work effort. Say no to unrelated activities if necessary. When you remain in calm control you can address other people's emergencies in a calm, controlled state as well.

"There is nothing so useless as doing efficiently that which should not be done at all." —Peter Drucker

WEEK 28: PERCEPTION

"The reverse side also has a reverse side."
—Japanese Proverb

We recognize the old saying 'there are two sides to every coin', but in life there are actually a myriad of sides to every story. And it becomes important to our success to be someone who can remain open to every perspective expressed.

I find in life that the direct and actively engaged individuals are always heard in a discussion and once they're done there is often a considerable amount of information on the table. I have to be cautious that I don't jump to the conclusion that everything that needs to be said has been without checking in with the more reserved individuals in attendance. I once bypassed the quietest member of the group over a series of meetings, landing on a solution that didn't work. Did the quiet demeanor mean this person didn't have something of value to contribute? No, she just couldn't get a word in edgewise. What about the solution that didn't work? She knew the solution was unlikely to work and had grounded reasoning behind her belief. But because I had not called upon her specifically, she was not granted the opportunity to give us her perspective of the situation and we lost a golden opportunity to get it right. The individual who never felt included ended up very frustrated with what she saw as a loss of effort for a flawed attempt to solve the problem. Lets remember to create the time needed to hear everyone's perspective and avoid unnecessary strain on the more introspective members of the team.

YOUR QUESTION THIS WEEK: How many perspectives are available to be expressed on any idea you have or situation you are addressing? (Hint: How many people are engaged in the conversation?)

YOUR ACTION STEP: Take one situation this week and use a group to offer their perspective on what the issue is, why it has occurred (root cause) and how it might be addressed. You'll find more options and combination of options for action than the number of people involved.

Example: A common exercise I like to use is to speak to a point 'from your side of the beach ball', holding the image of the colorful sections of a beach ball representing the different perspective of each individual in the room. Ensure everyone is given an opportunity to speak from his or her side of the beach ball.

"Every exit is an entrance somewhere else."
—Tom Stoppard

WEEK 29: PERFECTION

"Striving for excellence motivates you; striving for perfection is demoralizing."—Harriet Braiker

Once we accept that no person nor what they do will be perfect, we begin to develop confidence in stepping forward ourselves. It is in this understanding that people are not perfect that we develop compassion, including compassion for those that hold themselves back from pursuing their goals because they feel they don't know enough, won't be good enough, won't be perfect. So, whether you are sending a document draft back for the 10th revision or shaking your head at someone's work that doesn't meet your expectations, remember that something done is often better than nothing perfected.

> The quality of your work improves as a result of experience and learning.

Over time you will notice that not only the quality of your work improves as a result of experience and learning, but at the same time, that there is always another way to do or say something. As a result, your expectations of what would constitute 'perfect' will move up the scale as well. We seek to learn, we seek to improve, but as we move up the spiral of becoming our future selves, we cannot afford to hold back from our goals while we seek to demonstrate perfection.

YOUR QUESTION THIS WEEK: How many times do you hold back both yourself and others from moving something forward because you want it to be closer to your version of perfect? As you review your or someone else's work this week, can you stop yourself from seeking perfection?

YOUR ACTION STEP: With intention and purpose, let a piece of work be 'complete' instead of 'perfect' this week. It will feel uncomfortable but it will keep the energy and momentum moving forward.

"When you aim for perfection, you discover it's a moving target." —George Fisher

Chapter 5:
Achieve Results

"Moral excellence comes about as a result of habit. We become just by doing just acts, temperate by doing temperate acts, brave by doing brave acts."
—Aristotle

There are many ways that leaders encourage a culture of strong ethics and integrity. You will have many ways to put your stake in the sand by doing the 'right' thing. Although 'right' isn't always easy, your team will know, respect and trust you based on your history of making the 'right' decision in the face of being tempted to do what doesn't serve the greatest good. You will need to have courage to do the 'right' thing consistently but these acts reinforce with others the importance of doing things in a way that ensures fair and just behavior toward others, whether hiring practices or the use of resources among other equally important actions. Check in with your own integrity gauge. You will notice that the things that don't sit well with you, don't sit well with others either. No matter how small the situation appears, move into integrity by addressing it with openness and honesty, and, if needed, close with expectations for a different behavior or approach that leaves the whole team understanding you are doing the right thing for the right reasons.

Here's what I do: To test my planned action, I consider whether I would be proud to see it written on the front page of the newspaper tomorrow. Would it be the same treatment I would confer upon my family and friends? And would it be the action that I would expect to be taken on my own behalf?

YOUR QUESTION THIS WEEK: Is there a situation you know is out of integrity with the way you want yourself to be known? Have you avoided addressing it because you felt it would be easier to consider it as 'a small thing that will pass'?

YOUR ACTION STEP: Garner the support you may need to address a behavior or action that you know is out of integrity by applying the principles that you and your organization uphold. Take action this week to have it resolved.

Example: This may be meeting with an employee, may involve Human Resources or may require a conversation with your own mentor or manager.

> *"Character is doing the right thing when nobody's looking. There are too many people who think that the only thing that's right is to get by, and the only thing that's wrong is to get caught." —J.C. Watts*

WEEK 31: PRODUCTIVITY

"I'm a great believer in luck and I find the harder I work, the more I have of it." —Thomas Jefferson

Being productive takes a combination of things, most of which you have complete control over on any given day.

The first is to be organized and ready for the day. Know your calendar and what others are expecting of you before you begin and do that attitude check we practiced in Week 19, then commit to being focused for the day.

Next is to 'warm up' with a few quick and easy items that can be completed in under 30 minutes.

Third, focus on the most important goals for the day. Determine what are the 'must' completes before the 'want to' completes.

Fourth, eliminate distraction. I find the greatest distraction from being productive is continuous interruption. Block off your time and if you work in a shared office area or cubicle-land, you can take a laptop to a meeting room where you can work in quiet to make major strides forward without peripheral noise.

Fifth, schedule intermittent breaks of 10-15 minutes to work on email. Do not let it take over. You will find that there are many email strings that you may be copied on for information purposes but which may not need your direct comment, decision or action.

What's the cost of not being productive? You won't be getting your work out for others to see the value of your own contribution to the organization. Consider your contribution as a direct link to your value to the organization.

YOUR QUESTION THIS WEEK: Do you find yourself coming home tired and feeling like you didn't get anything done all day? Note these days and take 5 minutes to go back over your calendar to see where and how you spent your time. Review the five helpful hints above.

YOUR ACTION STEP: Begin a practice of tracking your time by categories.

Example: phone calls, meetings, task-based actions, e-Mail, mentoring others.

At the end of the week, tally up the totals in each category and take a fresh look at how you can block your time to achieve your highest level of focus and productivity.

> *"I've decided that the stuff falling through the cracks is confetti and I'm having a party!"*
> *—Betsy Cañas Garmon*

Chapter 6:
Your Comfort Zone

"Good decisions come from experience, and experience comes from bad decisions." —Author Unknown

Decision is the most important function of the mind. Nothing can occur until a decision is made. You can stay in the complacency of no decision but no idea will move forward without a decision. The decision is what triggers action. I've always been fascinated with people who are fearful of making a decision. Every decision isn't always seen as the 'right decision' once you are further down the road and looking back, but you won't actually know if it was the right decision until you enter into the string of actions that are spring boarded from that decision point. We can only make decisions based on what we know at a given moment in time and as actions unfold so does the iterative knowledge that comes from seeing the next step and the next step along the way. To make a decision, any decision, is to take the risk of being seen to be wrong. The truth is, no one is ever actually wrong; we simply make a decision based on what we know at that particular moment in time. The more we know about any situation the better our decision will be. Because of this variable, actual knowledge in the moment, a decision may not stand the test of time; it's simply a representation of a point in time. That's just fine. When new information arrives, an adjustment to correct the course you're on is always an acceptable action to take.

I've always been known to be a decision maker and I make a habit of letting people know that a decision I have made is not written in stone. Should there be more information, a change in contributing factors or if adverse results occur, I am open to further dialogue and reconsideration of the direction we are taking. This counters the tendency for yourself and others to consider a decision made in the harsh terms of right or wrong.

YOUR QUESTION THIS WEEK: Is there an outstanding decision you haven't made because you are afraid of making the wrong decision?

YOUR ACTION STEP: Make a decision. If there proves to be a need for course correction later, so be it. You will make a new decision at that point in time.

"In a minute there is time for decisions and revisions that a minute will reverse." —T.S. Eliot

WEEK 33: COURAGE

"You must do the things you think you cannot do."
—Eleanor Roosevelt

Any time we face something new our paradigms of fear arise to speak to us as a voice in our heads. The paradigm is a version of reason or belief that has been previously entered into our psyche. To do something different from that belief already implanted in our subconscious mind, we must do what may now seem unreasonable and therefore uncertain. Our comfort zone is a safe and predictable environment. It is filled with experience and people around you who are happy to never experience the disruption or instability brought on by change.

> Initiate the step into what may seem like darkness.

However, if you are ready to grow and expand your existence by making a choice for a new belief, a new plan of action, a change from previous experience, you will have to initiate the step into what may seem like darkness. The new act is simply beyond the light of your experience to date. As soon as you leave the outer edge of what you know, the next step will be illuminated for you, perhaps by a new circumstance, or other people and events that come into the situation. Face the unknown with courage, understanding you only need to get to the edge of the light you now know and take one step more.

I have had to draw on courage many times in my career. I have felt like I've been jumping off the edge of a cliff with many choices I have made along the way, including leaving a good paying job to meet a personal need, following the inner desire to start my own business, changing cities, choosing divorce, engaging with people who I perceived as being 'more' than me, whether it be more educated, more wealthy, more experienced or more connected in order to further my progress toward my own dreams. Courage for me is certainly like taking a hard swallow and jumping into the unknown.

YOUR QUESTION THIS WEEK: Is there something you have been procrastinating over? Do you feel that you need to dig deep to find courage to step into something new?

Hint: If it scares you it is worth doing.

YOUR ACTION STEP: First, write down the goal with clarity of image, shape, form and feeling. The clearer your image of the goal you wish to reach, the more energetically charged it becomes to attract the thoughts, the people and the energy you will need to accomplish it.

Second, list all the possible actions you could take to move you forward—baby steps count here.

Third, take action on one of those steps identified every day.

This will shift your fear and allow new ideas and energy to flow in, increasing your courage.

"We must build dikes of courage to hold back the flood of fear." —Martin Luther King Jr.

Chapter 7:
Change

"It takes a lot of courage to release the familiar and seemingly secure, to embrace the new. But there is no real security in what is no longer meaningful. There is more security in the adventurous and exciting, for in movement there is life, and in change there is power." —Alan Cohen

Understanding that we must find our own courage in order to create change, consider the impact that our change has on others around us. They didn't create the change, didn't ask for it, likely don't see the need for it and they are not the ones in the driver's seat. If you can help them see the future state, envision the good they will derive or the ease they will experience you will receive less resistance. When you help them see the reason for change you will pave the way for them to see the path you wish them to follow with you. Let's not forget that all change comes with an experience of grief as we let go of the old. It may be as small as the old office layout that allowed for a particular type of social exchange or something as significant as moving to a different office building, where adjustments have to be made to the patterns of commuting, parking, seating arrangements, lunch options and work colleagues. Changing work processes translates into losing something that someone is really good at, perhaps they're the office guru at doing something that was once seen as highly valuable to the organization. And now, it is no longer relevant. Change comes in many forms, and in many layers of intensity and impact.

It is important to me to remind myself during any change, no matter how minor, to carry a conscious awareness associated with its impacts on others. I am highly resilient to change, but not everyone is.

YOUR QUESTION THIS WEEK: What is an upcoming change, whether large or small, that you can help your peers or staff to adjust to by taking time to address their fears and perception of loss?

YOUR ACTION STEP: Initiate a conversation around a recent change to do a check-in with the people involved to discover where they are in the change process of grief (loss), acceptance or adoption.

Example: You can help someone move from being an unconscious competent through the conscious competent state of a 'newbie' by encouraging them to not see themselves as less capable but as a student of the future state, where they will once again be the master of a new process and be completely comfortable within a very short time.

"All changes, even the most longed for, have their melancholy; for what we leave behind us is a part of ourselves; we must die to one life before we can enter another." —Anatole France

WEEK 35: FLEXIBILITY

"If you don't like something change it; if you can't change it, change the way you think about it."
—Mary Engelbreit

Our thoughts lead to actions, our actions lead to habits, habits create our lives, as we know them. For many of us, the same, repetitive approach to living is boring or energy sapping. Breaking a habit can open our minds to be ready to entertain alternative ways to thinking about our work and our lives, bringing a new reenergized approach to what we do. We have the power within us to change our mind at any time, and that includes changing our thoughts, our actions and our plans.

I realize I drive my administrative assistant a little crazy by moving planning and task time around in the calendar to switch things up and use the natural flow of the day and my own peak times for productivity. I actively do simple changes in my commute and parking routine to reinforce (without dramatic action) that there are alternative ways to do all things.

Being comfortable and in a mindset of flexibility allows me to juggle many more subject areas, whether operational teams, projects or committees than I would likely be able to do if I did the same thing in the same way every day and rarely exercised the muscle of flexibility.

QUESTION FOR THIS WEEK: How often do you stop to notice how you think about or approach certain things? How often do you consciously try to change it? This week notice one thing you do that reflects a thought pattern you have held a long time that creates a habitual response to a situation.

Example: Perhaps it's the route you drive to work, or the fact that you drink 3 cups of coffee before 09: 00 a.m. or that you always take a dominant role in a meeting.

YOUR ACTION STEP: Give yourself permission to create flexibility in your life by changing one thing this week that has become a habit. Use disruption of your routine to bring a renewal of awareness and energy into place. Creating your own minor changes keeps you stay mentally flexible enough to glide into changes when they arrive from the outside.

"When we are no longer able to change a situation, we are challenged to change ourselves."
—Victor Frankl

WEEK 36: THE MAGIC IN ACCEPTANCE

"He who rejects change is the architect of decay. The only human institution that rejects progress is the cemetery." —Harold Wilson

One of the few things we cannot avoid is change. It is the nature of existence to have constant growth and renewal. But, we are not in control of every change that comes our way. Rather than allowing ourselves to get emotionally caught up in the process of change, we can learn to accept the constancy of change early on in our career. With acceptance of change comes a mind opened to opportunity.

When faced with an external circumstance that I have no direct control over, such as budget constraints or organizational policy, I start with an acceptance of the situation as it looks in the moment. This takes me from reaction (emotional) to response (logical), acceptance being a calmer place to begin the creative process. But, I am never resigned to the condition. From that point of acceptance, I begin to creatively look for viable alternatives to get me to where I plan to go.

YOUR QUESTION THIS WEEK: What is a change that you are facing in your work place right now? How emotionally invested are you? Do you find yourself feeling angry or worried, or excited for the change? Identify what emotion you have connected to the change at hand.

YOUR ACTION STEP: Try out one of my favorite exercises. Make two columns on your page. Write down each of your negative emotions associated with the change ahead. Then, beside each one, write what you would feel if you thought the opposite thought about the change. For example, if you are feeling angry about this current change write 'angry' in the left column. In the right column you might write that you would need to feel accepting to the change. Write accepting on the right. Work your way down all the feelings you have listed. Across from worried you might write excited.

Then, cut your list in half vertically. Take only the list of feelings from the right hand column and carry them in your pocket for the week. Pull out the list and read them every time you feel yourself reacting negatively to discussion related to the change. Read the list to yourself, stating to yourself that this change brings you acceptance, happiness and excitement, whatever the positive words are on your list. You will change the emotions you are connecting to in relation to the change to positive ones and begin to see the benefits of your positive acceptance far beyond the change itself.

"Change is the law of life. And those who look only to the past or present are certain to miss the future." —John F. Kennedy

Chapter 8:
Develop Yourself

"It is a thousand times better to have common sense without education than to have education without common sense." —Robert G. Ingersoll

I t has been proven to me many times over the years that formal education is not enough to create a success in business or any other aspects of your life. Understanding theory is interesting, having frameworks and tools in your pocket is useful, a strong work ethic can help you get through things when you aren't yet experienced enough to be efficient, but having common sense is the critical 'it factor' for success.

You will need to develop your ability to make good judgments on the fly and that requires what has been coined as 'common sense', an ability to accurately perceive the breadth of outcomes of any action, connecting the dots to potential reactions and understanding the impact of decisions you make.

> Common sense is the critical 'it factor' for success.

You can expand your knowledge daily through stories, facts, insights and ideas from both formal and informal studies, the books you read and the podcasts you listen to or the people you engage with.

Example: I have found that making time to receive information and input consistently builds an expanded matrix of reference from which I can answer questions and respond to future challenges using my own 'common sense'.

QUESTION FOR THIS WEEK: Do you find yourself surprised by the outcomes that result from decisions you have made, or the reactions of others to your choices?

YOUR ACTION STEP: Look for an opportunity to apply your 'common sense' to a question you find yourself facing. Then, with the purpose of expanding your reference points to the question, talk with someone else about whether they see the same 'common sense' approach and expected outcome as you do. If not, why not? What insights do they share with you?

I find that this exercise expands the number of reference points I have, shifting my current state of common sense to something broader, holding greater possibilities.

"In times of change, learners inherit the Earth, while the learned find themselves beautifully equipped to deal with a world that no longer exists." —Eric Hoffer

Week 38: Experience

"Experience is not what happens to a man. It is what a man does with what happens to him." —Aldous Leonard Huxley, Texts and Pretexts, 1932

Don't underestimate the power of experience. We learn by doing and adjusting and doing and adjusting and doing and adjusting. Those that have lived an experience before us have done more doing and adjusting than you will have time for. You will need to be able to pick up where your predecessor left off, so pick up their approach or an approach used by others with similar experience in seeking solutions.

When I was a young Manager, I created an opportunity to learn about effective meeting leadership. I asked to attend a specific meeting and offered to be the minute taker. This allowed me to gather the first level of experience in preparation and communication regarding meeting outcomes while listening and observing. When the Chair of the particular committee stepped down doe to other commitments, I then recommended we have a rotating Chair, allowing me to become an active leader in the meeting. I created the opportunity to gain the experience I needed to lead effective meetings. After four decades, I still express admiration to others who effectively lead difficult meetings as it is an art as much as a science, much of the skill coming from experience.

YOUR QUESTION THIS WEEK: Take 5 minutes alone with your thoughts and be honest. Ask yourself "What area of 'being' a leader do I need more experience in?"

Example: Is it labour relations, meeting management, engagement of others? Can you see one area where you lack confidence?

Hint: This is a subject area or skill set that you will increase from experience and more direct involvement.

YOUR ACTION STEP: This week, create the opportunity to engage in an experience you know could increase your abilities based on the area of interest you have targeted above. Reach out and find a way to learn and practice.

> *"Human beings, who are almost unique in having the ability to learn from the experience of others, are also remarkable for their apparent disinclination to do so." —Douglas Adams; Last Chance to See*

WEEK 39: SKILLS

"Skill to do comes of doing." —Ralph Waldo Emerson

There is no question that skills become one of your greatest assets in the workplace. How independently are you functioning today?

Some of my greatest skills development occurred the first time I left the corporate environment, and the team of people available to support my needs, to work as an independent consultant. Learning, not only how to complete the tasks at hand using the software tools available but to do so proficiently, directly impacted my ability to profit from the contracts I was committed to.

I've witnessed many staff over the years that don't have the proficiency with office productivity software that is designed to increase ease and efficiency in their day. We don't always have the luxury of a support team to execute on every task that faces us as a leader. Training is required no matter what level you are functioning at. Take the time to learn now what will save you time later.

YOUR QUESTION THIS WEEK: How strong are your practical skills using the software applications available on your computer?

YOUR ACTION STEP: Choose one software product function you would like to learn more about and spend 10 minutes each day this week to search for knowledge on a 'how to'.

Example: Using the standard Microsoft application suite, whether MS Word, MS Excel, Outlook Mail or Power Point, can save you hours in a day. You will find the equivalent running on the Mac platform. Each application has a powerful set of features to explore and apply.

Hint: You can check out software 'Help' links; look for a video on YouTube; ask a colleague how they learned the same skill, etc.

"A computer will do what you tell it to do, but that may be much different from what you had in mind." —Joseph Weizenbaum

WEEK 40: SELF AWARENESS

"Everyone thinks of changing the world, but no one thinks of changing himself." —Leo Tolstoy

It is easy to fall into the trap of thinking that changing everything outside of us could make our own life better. We have no control over what's outside of ourselves but we do have complete dominion over what we choose to do to grow and improve ourselves. When you become more self aware you instinctively begin to see aspects of your personality and behavior that you didn't notice before, aspects that you want to improve upon. No one wants to be seen as 'less than' what we believe others expect, but when we courageously shine the light of awareness on ourselves we must consider what unfair criticism we levy upon ourselves. Choosing positive behaviors like kindness, compassion, acceptance, respect, and honesty, our self awareness and emotional growth expand more quickly than if we choose old habits of perfection, judgment, criticism or ultimately rejection as we look at ourselves. Our increasing success is directly linked to our increasing self-awareness. Be kind to yourself as you look within and begin to increase your self-awareness.

YOUR QUESTION THIS WEEK: Can you see a moment when you have judged yourself harshly or in a negative way?

YOUR ACTION STEP: Every day this week, commit to taking 5 minutes to sit quietly in introspection. Each day, identify a moment in which you see how you could have chosen a different response toward yourself that would have felt less negative?

Express gratitude for the insight you have gained by increasing your awareness of your old beliefs and attitudes that can now be replaced with positive thoughts and appreciation for yourself.

Example: Part of my routine when I tuck myself into bed at night is to review how well I did that day in being the person I want to be. This takes a willingness to practice self-awareness and a loving look in the rear view mirror.

"Very often a change of self is needed more than a change of scene." —Arthur Christopher Benson

WEEK 41: OPEN MINDEDNESS

"It is impossible for a man to learn what he thinks he already knows." —Epictetus

Let's talk about the 'I know that' syndrome. When we listen to someone and are quick to respond with 'I know that', we are cutting off our mind from the potential of learning more deeply or seeing an experience from another perspective. Instead, when we carry a sense of curiosity with our encounters with others, we hear things differently.

When we are open to learning something new, and ask questions from an intention to expand or go deeper into the subject area, our mind is open to possibilities that we hadn't considered on our own.

I once thought I knew how an employee felt about her job. She was always grumpy, snapped at her coworkers and came in late. I had made up my mind that she hated her job and I needed to encourage her to look for something else as quickly as she could or I would have to let her go, impacting her more negatively. I arranged to meet with her for that purpose and entered into a dialogue that surprised us both. By expressing what I saw and asking her to tell me why she hated her job, I learned a very different story. She came in late because she wasn't sleeping due to the night care she was providing to her terminally ill mother. She snapped at her coworkers because she felt their complaints throughout their workday were 'petty' when compared with the life and death circumstance she faced at home with her mother each day. She actually loved the work and was grateful to have a job that used her skills and matched her training so well. Instead of setting the stage for firing her, I looked for ways to support her while she was going through her challenges at home. Taking the time to ask the question and be open-minded provided the opportunity for this individual to get through a difficult time in life and become a star employee thereafter.

YOUR QUESTION THIS WEEK: Do you ever listen with the 'I know that' syndrome veiling your opportunity to learn any new information on a familiar subject?

Example: Listen carefully to someone else's description of a problem that requires your analysis and action or solution.

YOUR ACTION STEP: Catch yourself bypassing what's being said and saying 'I know that' inside your head while listening to others this week. Refocus on the information being shared and formulate a question you can ask in order to deepen your understanding.

Example: You may think you know the problem but you don't know everyone else's perception of the problem. Be open-minded, you may just change your own mind about what the problem really is.

"True knowledge exists in knowing that you know nothing. And in knowing that you know nothing, that makes you the smartest of all." —Socrates

WEEK 42: PERSISTENCE

"The road to success is dotted with many tempting parking places." —Author Unknown

The majority of people are too quick to throw up their arms and walk away from their aspirations and goals. A few carry on despite the barriers to attaining their goal. These few are the outstanding achievers of the world like Ford, Carnegie, Jobs. If there was a brick wall across the path they were on, they found a way to go over it, under it or around it in order to reach their destination.

There are a few elements you require in order for you to stick with something, no matter what. These include a clearly defined goal, a passion about achieving the goal, and an unwavering belief that you will reach the goal.

When your goals resonate within you, when you love what you do and love the vision you see ahead, you will be persistent in taking the actions required to reach them.

Example: We don't have to struggle to think about someone we are in love with—the same should apply to a goal or dream you fall in love with. In this analogy, you can see that our goals can be just as easily kept on the top of our minds and reflected in our actions.

YOUR QUESTION THIS WEEK: Are you prepared to do whatever it takes to reach your goal? Can you stick with it when your faith falters?

YOUR ACTION STEP: Define one goal that lights you up; something you would love.

Create a clear image of that goal being reached, including the feelings you will have when you accomplish that goal—satisfaction, recognition, acknowledgment, pride or freedom.

Find the resonance; that place where you feel deeply and emotionally connected to the attainment of your goal. Each time you think of your goal, experience the feelings you have identified with the accomplishment of that goal. This will fire up your drive and persistence.

> *"Optimist: someone who figures that taking a step backward after taking a step forward is not a disaster, it's a cha-cha."* —Robert Brault

WEEK 43: HAPPINESS

"The essence of philosophy is that a man should so live that his happiness shall depend as little as possible on external things."—Epictetus

Happiness is an internal state of mind. We all have a 'set point' for happiness. This is a baseline that has come from our genetics, our upbringing, our environment and other conditions around us. Like a thermostat, we can be influenced (happier) when something happens that is perceived to be positive, but we generally settle into our set point once again. Research in positive psychology is providing us with proof that we are able to influence this set point for ourselves by consciously choosing to be happy. We can experience happy feelings in every experience, whether a great cup of coffee, a song on our playlist or a successful outcome at work. Happiness is very much in our control each and every day.

YOUR QUESTION THIS WEEK: Do you consciously take the 10-second opportunities in each day to acknowledge your state of happiness? Yes, it only takes 10 seconds or less.

Example: Catch yourself with a furrowed brow and switch to a smile. Look out a window and be happy to have the opportunity to work each day. Be happy

Raise the set point on your happiness thermostat.

we have cellular telephones available to make it easy to stay in touch with friends and family regardless of where we are.

YOUR ACTION STEP: Look for happiness in everything this week. Allow yourself to see something in every experience and every simple pleasure, to be grateful for. Then reinforce the happiness thought by physically smiling about it. I guarantee you will raise the set point on your happiness thermostat.

> *"If you observe a really happy man you will find him building a boat, writing a symphony, educating his son, growing double dahlias in his garden, or looking for dinosaur eggs in the Gobi desert. He will not be searching for happiness as if it were a collar button that has rolled under the radiator. He will not be striving for it as a goal in itself. He will have become aware that he is happy in the course of living life twenty-four crowded hours of the day."*
> *—W. Beran*

WEEK 44: IN YOUR CONTROL

"Things turn out best for the people who make the best out of the way things turn out." —Art Linkletter

It is common to think that we can have this or do that once something else has occurred. In other words, we are living in a reactive state rather than a creative state. If you were in control, would that change everything? Well you are. You are in complete control over your conditions, your experience of life and everything in it. The thing that controls our results is our belief in our current paradigms. Paradigms or beliefs are a form of myth. Only 500 years ago, mankind believed that the world was flat and that if someone went too far, he would fall off the edge of the earth. And, even if the world was round, they believed we would certain to fall off when we sailed around to the bottom of the curve. Without the knowledge of the earth's gravitational field, the human race lived a very small, confined existence.

We can redesign our results by redesigning our thinking, altering our beliefs. We can be more than the circumstances that surround us. Although it's not common thinking, we have power over our paradigms and are in control of the life we live. Paradigms are just old beliefs and patterns that we can stare down. And stare them down is what we will need to do in order to move beyond them to our goals. Don't think yourself foolish because you talk to yourself. Saying it out loud will strengthen your conviction and the message to your mind. You will be glad to tell those old beliefs that they no longer have a place at the front of your mind, you have a new belief now and you have a goal you will be accomplishing.

YOUR QUESTION THIS WEEK: Are there old myths that you believe in that are holding you back from your goals?

Example: Do you have old beliefs that people with money are selfish (and you don't want to be selfish) or that you're meant to be single (it's just not in your karma to find love in this life) or you're not the right person to reach that BHAG (big hairy audacious goal) (there's someone else more qualified or deserving)? Whatever the belief statement you hear yourself saying or thinking, you are in control of changing those thoughts, and in turn, changing your beliefs.

YOUR ACTION STEP: Take control. Turn to your passion to stoke the fire you feel for your goal and reinforce your new belief system that will support your goal state.

Check—Check your thinking. Am I tuned into the myths of my upbringing instead of my goals? You may have had those thoughts 'up until now' but you can choose to no longer believe them.

Protect—As soon as you notice that fear or worry or doubt are coming into your thoughts, protect your dream. The only person who opens the door to fear, doubt and worry when they knock is you. Acknowledge them for what they are—old beliefs—and send them away as quickly as they appear.

Connect—There is something in this moment that you can do to step closer to your goal.

There is something within you that is more powerful than anything outside of you. Build the new beliefs necessary to carry you to your goals.

> *"What you're supposed to do when you don't like a thing is change it. If you can't change it, change the way you think about it. Don't complain." —Maya Angelou*

WEEK 45: HEALTH

"Diseases can be our spiritual flat tires—disruptions in our lives that seem to be disasters at the time but end by redirecting our lives in a meaningful way."
—Bernie S. Siegel

Health is often the most obvious area where our life is reflected. I've had two major health scares in my life, both requiring medical intervention and time off work. Obviously a slow learner, I insisted on pushing myself to the point of needing to be hit over the head with the proverbial 2x4 more than once. Taking my body for granted, I experienced two diagnoses and treatment plans, years apart, which required recovery time and a reframe of what I could do to support my personal health. We cannot ignore our health without paying a price.

While the human body can send subtle, consistent messages to us, we often choose to ignore these due to what we perceive to be more pressing issues at hand.

Here's what I've learned:

- Although resilient, the human body is not a machine

- Your body requires maintenance, including food, water, exercise and rest

- Your body is infinitely intelligent and adaptive

- Your body is an honest communicator of what you are doing right and doing wrong, if you are willing to listen to it

- Only you can take care of your body.

YOUR QUESTION THIS WEEK: What is your body telling you about itself this week?

Examples: Do you feel rested, hydrated, energized? Or do you feel tired, congested and lethargic? Are all systems functioning well? Are your muscles flexible and strong?

YOUR ACTION STEP: Take 2 minutes each day to listen to your body and recognize the subtle messages it may be sending you. Listen and take action. Whether physical, mental or spiritual in nature, take action. Only you can take care of your health.

"If I'd known I was going to live so long, I'd have taken better care of myself." —Leon Eldred Wolfe

WEEK 46: IT'S A MARATHON, NOT A SPRINT

"The bad news is, time flies like an arrow. The good news is you hold the bow." —Anonymous

Life is not a sprint, it's a marathon and you will need to pace yourself accordingly. When you complete an assignment, you may be pushing in a sprint. But when you set larger goals, whether for a project, your career, or your life, ensure you give yourself enough time to be successful and to enjoy the process. You've heard it before—"Life isn't a destination, it's a journey".

In my life, I have skipped over the celebratory moments in my career. Things I never stopped to acknowledge at the time they occurred include promotions, winning contracts, writing strong business proposals that resulted in multimillion dollar projects, graduations. In recent years I have learned to celebrate almost everything, completion of a certification, buying a new car, purchasing a home.

In the past, I have made the mistake of framing each event in life as a series of 'actions'. Picking up the new car might have been boiled down to the intellectual steps of making the selection, obtaining a loan, signing off the paper work, scheduling of the appoint for pick up, getting the parking card, literally just another 'to do' item in life. All that has changed. Now, getting a new car is about the excitement of the fact that the perfect car for me was right there waiting, the color is exactly what I wanted, the interior is aesthetically beautiful, the smell and feel of the soft new leather is a luxury and this car represents a reward for my hard work that earned the dollars to pay for it. Like any other accomplishment in life, it deserves recognition and can be expressed through feelings of gratitude. I now take the day to really celebrate this new car as part of my life and my life journey, not relegating it a simple series of steps to complete the goal.

YOUR QUESTION THIS WEEK: Are you racing through your days without noticing the beauty of the journey?

Example: Are you noticing the people you meet along the way this week? Are events a part of the mass of work you do without you acknowledging they may be important to both you and other people in more meaningful ways than simply something done?

YOUR ACTION STEP: This week, you will slow your pace, moving from frantic to methodically steady. Think of it as a pace on the treadmill where you can comfortably look around from side to side and still speak to others while running.

We are on a long and important journey of self-discovery and fulfillment. Let's acknowledge and enjoy the markers along the road.

"Every man is a damn fool for at least five minutes every day; wisdom consists in not exceeding the limit." —Elbert Hubbard

Week 47: Gratitude

"We often take for granted the very things that most deserve our gratitude." —Cynthia Ozick

Much is written about the power of gratitude and yet we can race into our day and fall into bed at night without taking time to express gratitude for all that has been brought to us. People, actions, opportunities and outcomes for which we can be grateful surround us. Taking time to acknowledge our gratitude is often like the secret sauce that is missing from our life. Happiness, peace and success have all been contributed to consistent observation of the good in life and the act of expressing a loving gratitude for it.

YOUR QUESTION THIS WEEK: Do you stop at least once a day to express gratitude for all that you have in your life?

YOUR ACTION STEP: Express verbally or in writing the gratitude you feel for all that is in your life each day this week.

Example: This might include your family and friends, the home you live in, the car you drive, the money in the bank, the job you have, the people you work with and the opportunities that flow to you, even a hard lesson you've learned.

Hint: If you do this before falling to sleep at night, you will have a deeper, more restful sleep.

"The struggle ends when the gratitude begins." —Neale Donald Walsch

Chapter 9:
LOVE YOUR LIFE as a LEADER

"I saw the angel in the marble and carved until I set him free." —Michelangelo

I t was Einstein that taught us that 'everything is energy; that's all there is'. Our lives are the result of our thoughts and actions. Our ideas are a currency of the quantum universe. What we think and what we passionately believe, matched with what we feel in relation to those ideas, is what moves into form in this quantum energy field we live in.

You may have heard the saying 'the harder you work the luckier you get' but you'll easily enjoy any positive outcome if your thoughts and actions have been associated with doing what you love.

I set this up by thinking thoughts each day that are consistent with the outcome I desire. Taking positive action each day creates the energy needed to bring my thoughts into form to support me in reaching a goal I am passionate about.

YOUR QUESTION THIS WEEK: Do you think about the future you desire once a day?

YOUR ACTION STEP: Direct your thoughts on living in your vision or goal once each day. That's all, just once each day. Then get back to the here and now and take action. Keep your thoughts positive and focused on reaching your goals.

"The universe is transformation; our life is what our thoughts make it." —Marcus Aurelius

WEEK 49: IMAGINATION

"First say to yourself what you would be; and then do what you have to do." —Epictetus

Do you remember what you were like when you were a child? How each day could be an adventure into a new existence? One day a farmer, then a teacher, perhaps an astronaut? Our education system trains our imagination out of us. We are told not to 'daydream', told 'don't be silly' or 'you can't do that'.

Leave that behind. Allowing your adult self to go back to your imagination is a joyful experience to be repeated often. The imagination is a powerful mental faculty that is the first stage of the creative process. Everything that exists began in someone's imagination, a seed of the thought. A seed of thought leads to goals that require planned actions to achieve. Imagine the idea of moon landings, cellular phones, communicating by email were sheer fantasy only a few decades ago.

Napolean Hill wrote, that the imagination is literally the workshop wherein all plans are created. The impulse, the desire, is given form by the imaginative faculty of your mind. Without realizing it, we rehearse everything in our imagination before it comes into form.

You can use your imaginative mental faculty to discover that all things are possible. If the real currency in life is the ideas that come from our imagination, then have fun and exercise the freedom of your imagination. Once you have an idea, you can consider and calculate with your intelligence. When you bring these two together, you will set goals for the path to make the idea a reality.

I've actively used my imagination all my life. When I was began to work part time while in high school, I would imagine what it would be like to earn enough money to buy shoes whenever I saw a pair that would match my wardrobe. I imagined the type of car I would own, the color and size. I could see myself washing and waxing it. My imagination created my self-image as a best selling author. I used my imagination to define the location, design and interior furnishings of the condominium apartment I live in. My imagination is employed full time in the creation of my future and so is yours. Use it to seed thoughts of your future.

YOUR QUESTION THIS WEEK: Is there an outcome you desire that you could use your imagination to design? What's the fantasy outcome you could create?

YOUR ACTION STEP: Now begin to build wonderful pictures in your mind using your imagination. Design your future with the use of your imagination. Once you have the idea designed in your mind then you can bring it into the present state and apply the logical mind to its creation in form. To do this, you can simply ask your creative mind, 'What next step can I take today to accomplish this outcome?' New ideas will pop into your mind with surprising regularity.

"Map out your future, but do it in pencil." —Jon Bon Jovi

WEEK 50: FORGIVENESS

"There's no point in burying a hatchet if you're going to put up a marker on the site." —Sydney Harris

When we don't consciously forgive a person, circumstance or outcome, we are held hostage to it. When we hold onto a resentment or grudge it's like picking up a hot coal to throw it at another but in the end realizing that it's you who picked it up that gets most severely burned. Is there someone you need to forgive? Think of forgiveness while in the shower each day. Let the water flow over you and wash away your resentment, anger or grudge.

Example: I was once harrassed at a new job by a bitter employee who had thought she would be promoted to the job I was hired into. The first month on the job I began to receive numerous hang up phone calls late at night. This went on for a few weeks until I finally heard backgound noise with an overhead speaker paging someone. I recognized this as the paging system at the hospital I was working at. Then, a second clue exposed a phone number that was the main office

> When we don't consciously forgive a person, circumstance or outcome we are held hostage to it.

number in the deparment I was responsible for. I told my boss and reported the incidents to Security. I had been watching quietly for behavioural clues at the office, and noticed the lack of eye contact combined with avoidance by one individual, so I engaged. I told her my story about how I was receiving a series of late night phone calls that I had now discovered as coming from the hospital. The individual turned pale in front of my eyes and asked if I could tell where the calls were made from. When I indicated I didn't know which phone but I knew it was within our department and had reported the situation to Security to await an investigation, the calls suddenly stopped and I didn't have further investigation undertaken. It didn't take too many months for this individual to feel uncomfortable enough at being found out that she found employment elsewhere. It was about three years later that I saw a photo of this individual in a 'print ad' for a hospital on the other side of the country. Those suppressed feelings of anger and hurt came flooding in and the pain in the pit of my stomach told me that it was time to let it go.

The personal lesson I learned was that I carried both hurt and anger about this individual's behaviour toward me for far too long.

The business lesson I took from this was to ask my employers who the internal candidates were that competed for any position I was granted so that I could ensure I openly acknowledged them in a private conversation and build a direct and positive relationship with them from the first week onward. I undertook this relationship buiding exercise in every promotion and job I ever took in the decades following. I now allow no room for underground feelings and address issues head on, whether with another individual, or with the help of a third party.

YOUR QUESTION THIS WEEK: Is there something you need to let go of or someone from the past that you need to forgive?

YOUR ACTION STEP: Glean the learning from the situation and choose not to carry resentment forward as baggage in your life. Think of the person you need to forgive and, holding their image in your mind, say three times "I wish you well, I wish you well, I wish you well".

> *"To forgive is to set a prisoner free and discover that the prisoner was you." —Lewis B. Smedes, Forgiveness—The Power to Change the Past*

WEEK 51: PATIENCE

"Patience is a most necessary qualification for business; many a man would rather you heard his story than granted his request." —Lord Chesterfield

It is true that we acquire patience with age. If for no other reason but that we see how impatience can be damaging. All life moves forward at a natural pace. When we are attuned to a natural rhythm within us and around us, we too can learn the pace of patience. As a leader, we find our patience less stretched as we learn more about the human experience and the importance of patience in compassion for both others and ourselves. It is through patience that we discover the richness of insight that lies just beneath the surface of most things whether related to an idea, a person or a circumstance.

As a creator, I often feel an urgency to act. It is as if my vision will evaporate if I don't get it into real form quickly. At times, it feels like pure will that strengthens my ability to remain patient for the outcome I know is possible. I know that patience will eventually reveal all that is necessary for success.

Patience has been a life-long lesson for me. I've spent decades approaching my life as a race against time, fitting in as much as I possible can at any moment in time; as much reading, as much education, as much travel, as much work. . . you name it. Perhaps if I'd had more patience, and allowed things to unfold more naturally, I'd have had less need for the 2x4 mentioned in Week 45. I've worked very hard to become more patient in all aspects of my life. Raising a child helped with that, but I will add that an acceptance of what I cannot control or the acceptance of a circumstance, such as the prolonged process for government approval of budget funding, goes a long way to reinforce the need for a state of patience with oneself as well as with other people's pace and process.

To be fully transparent on this, I still approach every day with a hard push to accomplish as much as possible. I think I'm hard wired for that. But, I do it with slightly more patience for others who are riding the train with me.

YOUR QUESTION THIS WEEK: Are you feeling impatient about an outcome while you wait for a decision by another?

YOUR ACTION STEP: Sit with your positive thoughts for 3 days before checking back on something you are waiting for. After 3 days make contact, but request a status report with a voice of patient understanding, knowing that your urgency may not be the other individual's urgency at this time. As always close the contact with a thank you for their response.

"Adopt the pace of nature: her secret is patience."
—*Ralph Waldo Emerson*

WEEK 52: SUCCESS

"You cannot be anything you want to be—but you can be a lot more of who you already are."
—Tom Rath

If you're a follower of the positive psychology movement and of the development of strengths-based performance, you will understand the quote above.

Understanding who you really are, acknowledging your gifts and talents, and working consistently on strengthening these will set you on the path to creating noticeable qualities that evidence your suitability to any work you pursue. As a leader, you will find that the more you build on your strengths, the easier it will be to realize success and build upon those strengths in future endeavors. The same is true for those around you.

You will find that your definition of success is ever changing. It is human nature to climb the mountain peak you see, only to see a higher peak once you stand atop the last. As you move upward in the rising spiral of success, use your learning and growth to help others on the climb below you. There is sweetness in the experience of success when it is shared in ways that support others. The natural strengths and talents of those you work with will be different than yours and each individual will benefit from the unique line of sight that you are able to provide.

In my current role I designed a new functional model with a variety of new service areas, then a new organizational structure to go with it. I was certainly successful in completing the task and, through that, reaching the goal. But the real success has been demonstrated many times over as the individuals engaged in the new structure have been able to successfully create the most unique, highly functioning organization of its kind across the nation. Helping others see possibilities is key to my personal success.

QUESTION FOR THIS WEEK: What is a success you have experienced that can help someone else based on the experience, the learning and the unique perspective you brought to the situation.

YOUR ACTION STEP: Look for the strengths in those around you this week; help each individual be successful through their natural strengths, skills and talents. Success shared becomes your legacy.

> *"Success you have shared becomes a valued inheritance to others." —Karanne Lambton*

CLOSING THOUGHTS:

"I have learned, that if one advances confidently in the direction of his dreams, and endeavors to live the life he has imagined, he will meet with a success unexpected in common hours." —Henry David Thoreau

I hope you have gained both confidence and skill by being inspired each week to consider the questions I have asked and to work through the ideas and actions I have proposed.

My own success has been built on a platform of continuous learning and growth, with a great deal gained from the informal education received through experience and relationships in the workplace. What I have learned from my leaders, coaches, colleagues and my staff over the years is beyond measure, and I know that as I continue to grow and mentor, more learning lies ahead.

When we take time to live an inspired life we not only witness our own transformation but also the impact we have on others around us. To couple that with a consciousness for learning, gives us an opportunity to improve our self and as a result, increase the value of our contribution every

> Every day is a good day to make small improvements in your effectiveness as a leader.

day. Wake up each day inspired and go to bed each night with gratitude. You will not only succeed as a leader, you will delight in who you become along the way. Every day is a good day to make small improvements in your effectiveness as a leader. Leaders are learners first. May you continue to learn, to grow and to succeed.

YOUR FINAL QUESTION: Have you experienced personal growth this year? In what ways?

YOUR ACTION STEP: Write down your personal successes and . . . Celebrate!

"Though no one can go back and make a brand new start, anyone can start from now and make a brand new ending." —Author Unknown

ABOUT THE AUTHOR

A recognized, visionary and innovative leader in the health care industry, Karanne Lambton has been inspiring individuals and organizations to think big and realize their goals for over 35 years. She is the founder of Life Fulfilled Coaching and the principle of its parent company e-HRM Consulting Inc. Karanne has served as a corporate senior leader in strategic transformation, organizational design and health information management. Karanne has consulted for numerous organizations and spoken internationally on a variety of subjects, including visioning, strategic program development, organizational design and leadership. She is a certified Life Mastery Consultant who coaches corporate leaders, managers and employees using a proven 3-pillar process to elevate themselves, their career, their organization and their communities to new levels of success.

To contact Karanne visit
www.lifefulfilled.com

22007612R00089

Made in the USA
San Bernardino, CA
17 June 2015